W9-BQY-734

The following books are titles in the
Controversies in Education Series, Editorial Board
THE UNIVERSITY OF MASSACHUSETTS SCHOOL OF EDUCATION

Cooper—DIFFERENTIATED STAFFING

Hicks and Hunka—THE TEACHER AND THE COMPUTER

Lacey—SEEING WITH FEELING Film in the Classroom

Gentry, Jones, Peelle, Phillips,
Woodbury and Woodbury—URBAN EDUCATION: The Hope Factor?

Mallan and Hersh—NO G.O.D.'s IN THE CLASSROOM: Inquiry into
Inquiry

Mallan and Hersh—NO G.O.D.'s IN THE CLASSROOM: The Use of
Elementary Social Studies

Mallan and Hersh—NO G.O.D.'s IN THE CLASSROOM: The Use of
Secondary Social Studies

SEEING WITH FEELING
Film in the Classroom

RICHARD A. LACEY

Assistant Program Officer,
The Ford Foundation

1972
W. B. SAUNDERS COMPANY
PHILADELPHIA · LONDON · TORONTO

W. B. Saunders Company: West Washington Square
Philadelphia, Pa.   19105

12 Dyott Street
London, WC1A   1DB

1835 Yonge Street
Toronto 7, Ontario

It is too clear and so is hard to see.
A man once searched for fire with a lighted lantern.
Had he known what fire was,
He could have cooked his rice much sooner.

Zen poem

PREFACE

The Zen poem at the beginning of this book isn't meant to imply that movies are the answer to our problems in education, or even the most essential alternative teaching material available, despite what some converts maintain. But movies can work wonders in many classes and have profoundly influenced the lives of many schools. My most memorable, heady moments in and out of the classroom, with kids from nearly every kind of background, have been with movies. Working with movies had a great deal to do with changes in my personal style of teaching, and I hope in this book I communicate some of the reasons behind those changes.

My recent work in facilitating redesign of schools and school systems — helping teachers, principals, superintendents, parents, and kids develop options to conventional schooling — has convinced me that the whole film and multi-media movement is really a signal that many people want alternatives to what we now have and that they're willing to work within the system to create them. Dreary headlines to the contrary, I'm encouraged by what I see.

You may read this book with a grain of salt, especially when I supply recipes that sound sure-fire. However, as you read the book, ask yourself, not, "Yes, but will it really work for me?" Rather, ask, "How can I find a way to try it — or try something of my own that this suggests?" Also, as you read, think of other teachers or administrators who might be interested, or write me in care of the publisher with your comments, or use the special form at the end of the book if someone before you hasn't used it already (I'd feel good knowing this book gets dog-eared, coffee-stained, underlined, passed around). If something works, or if you think it might work, don't keep it a secret.

What I have discovered is that nothing — no particular film, no particular technique — "works." Movies are an occasion for an educational encounter, and whatever you and the kids do with that chance to make fresh honest contact is what does or does not work. This is why I would be disappointed if teachers tried to use this book as a cookbook.

Three sections of the text are developed in part from articles: "Documenting Truth as Well as Fact," *Independent School Bulletin,* February, 1968; "Whaddya Do When the Lights Go On?" *Media and Methods,* November, 1969; and an article to be published, written with Albert Furbay, on developing small support groups.

Special thanks —

To Wellington Grimes, The National Association of Independent Schools, and the Braitmayer Foundation for providing a grant for me to conduct much of my work toward this book.

To David Sohn, who got me started in film study and remained a close friend.

To Charles Boos, who was generous in providing films and laughs.

To Bell and Howell, who provided a magnificent projector for the work.

To Guy Simonelli, whom I thought I was going to teach, but who taught me so much about how to learn with kids.

To Susan Rice, for saying I'm funnier than the book.

To Virginia Cole, who cared.

And to a lot of kids, especially my own, Lydia and Eleanor, who constantly remind me what education is really about.

RICHARD A. LACEY

CONTENTS

Chapter 1

MOVIES: GIMMICK OR GODSEND?..................................... 1

Chapter 2

WHAT TO DO WHEN THE LIGHTS GO ON?...................... 11

Chapter 3

IMAGE-SOUND SKIMMING: IN-SIGHT 26

Chapter 4

BAG IS GAB SPELLED BACKWARDS: A DOZEN DEVICES... 55

Chapter 5

"YES, BUT!" 88

Chapter 6

A LITTLE HELP FROM MY FRIENDS 99

Appendix I

BOOKS ON FILM, FILM STUDY, AND CLOSELY RELATED
  TOPICS... 107

Appendix II

THE LITERATURE ON CHANGE, AND REFERENCES FOR SUPPORT
GROUPS 108

Appendix III

PERIODICALS ON FILM AND FILM STUDY................................ 109

Appendix IV

DISTRIBUTORS OF FILMS MENTIONED IN TEXT 110

Appendix V

SOME 16 MM. FILM DISTRIBUTORS 113

Appendix VI

FORM FOR READER'S COMMENTS TO AUTHOR........................ 118

1

MOVIES: GIMMICK OR GODSEND?

Pauline Kael[1] put it most bluntly: "If you think movies can't be killed, you underestimate the power of education." Her remark offended many struggling movie teachers, but it was apt. Exciting and rewarding as movies may be, they will not make any lasting, critical impact unless our schools and teachers are willing to consider new assumptions and ground rules as well as several interesting new techniques. If teachers will not behave differently and persuade others to join them, then movies will join the long and dusty shelf of short-lived gimmicks.

We must be willing to use movies in a way totally different from the customary approach of audio-visual education—the teaching of subjects by use of canned lectures or supplementary "enrichment" films—and we must also use totally fresh techniques of teaching. For many teachers this means clarifying and sometimes drastically revising educational aims and altering roles in the classroom. For those of us who are satisfied with our aims, it may mean re-examining how we are trying to achieve them.

Of course, teachers may use movies in many ways, and since standard teaching methods sometimes achieve deceptively quick successes with films, teachers are bound to seize upon them; they already have, in droves. Like medicine, though, movies can cause insidious harm if used improperly, and inevitably some teachers distort the value of films in the interest of injecting energy into their classes. With dyspepsia so prevalent in the schools, anyone who objects to this motive comes off as a purist, and perhaps deservedly.

We cannot afford to waste energy being watchdogs over film study, but we can constantly clarify our own purposes and provide inviting alternatives for colleagues who would like to change but

---

[1]Pauline Kael, one of the best-known film critics in the country, is one of the most acerbic critics of media education. She publishes criticism regularly in *The New Yorker* and has written books on film criticism: e.g., *I Lost It At the Movies*, and *Kiss Kiss, Bang Bang* (see Appendix I).

who are unsure how to begin. Before starting, though, we must distinguish between stopgap successes and ultimate aims.

We rarely think of movies as a legitimate or essential area of study. Movies are constantly justified as means to ends already established by traditional subjects. The difficulty with the approach used by liberal English, social studies, and humanities departments that include film as a means of acknowledging many forms of artistic communication is that acknowledgment, like lip service, is insufficient to promote growth.

FILM EDUCATION

Throughout this book I advocate several concepts governing film education. Particularly, a film educator should teach children, rather than any particular subject matter or even the qualities of the medium itself. More precisely, a film educator should help children learn how to learn, how to respond sensitively and effectively to others, how to clarify their sense of who they are, and how to develop capacities to choose freely from a variety of alternatives — all in relation and response to the screen. A film educator should foster these aims rather than the acquisition of particular skills or knowledge, valuable as such tools may be.

Often, film study stresses studying film language, film technique, filmmaking, and the use of film to illuminate other topics and issues. Although these may be occasionally important components of film study programs, they are secondary and tertiary uses of film. The primary concern of a film program (and of this book) is contact between the child and the film, and thus between the child and self, others, and the environment.

This may seem a large mouthful, and I cite it in order to convey the spirit of the enterprise. In later chapters I shall explain how these concepts operate.

A HUMANISTIC APPROACH

Recently we have been focusing our attention on how education might provide new, more humanistic, responsive learning environments. Film study, a promising beginning, is part of a widening movement toward sensitivity training in its broadest possible meaning: using and sharpening all of the senses, acknowledging and dealing with feelings as well as ideas, and becoming increasingly open to possibilities in experiencing, learning, and growing.

This humanistic approach to education and particularly to the use of film means that our classroom activities should concentrate upon the child's perceptions and his growing sense of self. These should, in fact, be the real content of the curriculum. Film, in my view, should be a stimulus to enable the student to examine the self—the sense of identity, of relatedness to others, and of potency.

The development of a sense of identity is at the heart of the psychology of film response. When we see a movie and empathize with characters or respond to situations, we temporarily adopt new roles. In various ways, the process of experimenting with unfamiliar roles is how we grow psychologically. Through trying on and selecting different behaviors we extend our repertoire of possible responses to situations we might encounter.

In addition, assuming various roles is the process by which we establish a sense of connectedness with others. Since this sense grows from empathy, the film experience is one kind of contribution to the process by which a student develops his awareness of being part of the human community.

Finally, the film experience can contribute to a student's sense of potency, particularly his ability to develop his own standards of judgment, to rely upon the validity of his own way of perceiving, and to become open and secure enough to accept other ways of perceiving.

FILM IS NOT ALONE

In case this discussion suggests that film educators and traditional teachers must be enemies, let me dispel that notion immediately. Since film study has acquired a tinge of anti-intellectual radicalism in the past few years, some sense of restraint is especially important here. Traditional teachers can become excellent film teachers. In fact, the solid, traditional teacher (and I include math and science teachers) may be able to teach film much more effectively than his "groovier" colleague. What is important is to be "groovy" with substance.

Contrary to popular misconception, a good film educator is not opposed to reading and writing; instead, he sees these activities as valuable tools. In fact, all traditional academic pursuits may be used to provide further insights into a student's experience of a film, so long as examining the experience rather than answering the academic questions receives the emphasis.

For instance, a student needs to be able to organize his ideas and feelings about a film coherently and cogently; this requires traditional classroom skills. Because he may synthesize other criticisms, background research, and his own feelings and ideas, he may be stimulated to refine his classroom skills in order to communicate accurately. Finally, in making a film or a videotape, he must be able to use three languages: written English, spoken English, and the language of film. All of these traditional activities and skills may be useful in examining a shared film experience, provided they do not become ends in themselves.

Even within the realm of film study, a film educator may teach the "language," history, and production of film, but such areas should never become paramount. A film educator's purpose is to help students to discover and share their particular ways of perceiving, to develop their own standards of judgment, and to express themselves in fresh ways by using the available technology.

I do not want to suggest, by defending traditional classroom concerns, that traditional teaching cannot ruin movies. It definitely can. The purpose of this book is to provide some approaches for *all* teachers to use in expanding their own repertoires of behavior, so that even though they may feel most comfortable in a traditional framework, they can also work effectively in unconventional situations. Most of the rhetoric about virtues of traditional vs. untraditional teaching is exactly that—rhetoric. No one has shown unequivocally what effective teaching is, but the most convincing evidence indicates that an effective teacher is one who is flexible, who is comfortable using a wide variety of behaviors, and who can be what he must be at a given moment. Therefore, I hope that the procedures described here will not only help all teachers to use film effectively but will provide them with viewpoints and approaches that they can apply in other situations as well.

SUBSTANCE AND FORM

The story of film study during the past few years underlines the problem of being progressive with substance. The promotion of film study by John Culkin, David Sohn, Anthony Hodgkinson, David Powell, David Mallery,[2] and others; numerous regional and

---

[2]John Culkin, originally an English teacher, is the pioneering figure in the film movement in schools and began the first National Film Conference for teachers, which he still conducts. In 1968 he directed the National Film Study Project at Fordham University, and now directs the Center for Understanding Media in New York City. (*Footnote continued on page 5.*)

national conferences; the establishment and substantial contribution of the American Film Institute; and the encouraging national response to *Media and Methods* magazine[3] have convinced many people that movies can be valuable in the classroom. A growing number claim that film is at least as important as print, not merely supplemental. *Media and Methods* proclaimed on its cover over three years ago, "The Film is *IN*—the classroom!"

At the same time, though, skeptics mutter, "Don't look now, but there goes one of those horrid audible-visible people." The heady talk of turning kids on with film has been too easy, and some of the results have not lived up to the advertising. Many devotees seem far better versed in McLuhan and Culkin than in specific ways movies can be used successfully. Often, few seem to know what to do with film in the less rarefied air of the daily classroom. They wonder what to do when the lights go on.

It is easy to agree when Stanley Kauffman[4] says, "The film in this country is possibly the one art form that is *wanted*." But how do we turn the excitement generated by film into learning? And learning what?

Carl Sandburg's answer, that all movies good or bad are educational and that Hollywood is a more effective educational institution than Harvard, is not an exaggeration. Similarly, many teachers have begun to realize that a medium which has shaped our tastes, interests, and habits of perceiving for so long has earned a place in the curriculum. Probably the most widely accepted reasoning is that students should become cinemate as well as literate.

(*Footnote 2, continued.*) David Sohn is Coordinator of Language Arts in District 65, Evanston, Illinois. He is coauthor with Hart Leavitt of *Stop, Look, and Write*, which uses photographs to teach composition. He has written or edited many books and has published countless articles on film and composition.

Anthony Hodgkinson, one of the earliest to articulate the need to use film in schools, wrote *Screen Education* (see Appendix I) and is presently associate professor of film education at Clark University in Worcester, Massachusetts.

David Powell is one of the prominent figures in film study in the northeastern United States. Powell has promoted systematic approaches to, and has conducted frequent conferences in, film study.

David Mallery is a member of the American Film Institute and Director of Studies for the National Association of Independent Schools. He has authored a number of well-known publications, among which are *Film in the Life of the Schools*, and *Schools and the Art of Motion Pictures* (see Appendix I).

[3]See Appendix III for a listing of names and addresses of periodicals on film and film study.

[4]Stanley Kauffman, a prolific film critic, has written books on film criticism and has published regularly in *The New Republic*.

Although television differs from film, the average viewer sees most movies on TV, and TV undeniably has a profound impact on the way we think and feel, the way we see the world. "Screen education," a term that includes both TV and film, has gained wide acceptance in the past few years, and its advocates maintain that since students spend more time watching TV than going to school (and now some people spend more hours watching TV than working), the schools should not fight the inevitable but should use this chance to educate students in responding to all media as sensitively and as perceptively as possible. At least we are beginning to heed, on paper and in public, McLuhan's warning that we are experiencing information overload, and that for students to be able to judge and select, they must be taught how to read the myriad codes used in communicating. Not long ago this sophistication, like artistic skill, was considered a frill. Now it has survival value, but we are still unaccustomed to considering it critical. Desirable as it may be, it remains subordinate to "basic" educational courses. As William Schuman[5] replied to those who claim that the arts have finally gained rightful status in the schools, "The frill is gone, but the malady lingers on."

HOW TO REACH THEM

It is a serious malady, too. All affective education, including film study, will always have second-class status unless teachers and schools begin to change their priorities and address the needs of the whole child—his feelings as well as his thoughts—in a systematic way. Even if screen education has gained a foothold, it will not be able to address the fundamental issues surrounding educational aims if teachers continue to stress grades, "right" answers, analytical but not expressive behavior, and the primacy of print.

The interest and excitement surrounding movies has moved teachers to think about the regular business of schools in fresh ways. Frequently they say that movies have shown them how to reach kids who resist everything else. It has also challenged sacred cows like the grading system, the structure of the classroom, the conventional ideas about how we learn, and the teacher's role. In discussing film study, then, we must examine how we as teachers learn, as well as how students learn. We must ask at

---

[5]William Schuman is former president of Lincoln Center in New York City.

the same time whether we are really serious about valuing freedom in learning. Do we really want curious, lively students who challenge assumptions and who increasingly direct their own learning? If so, what are we doing to encourage them to grow this way, how can movies help us, and what other strategies do films suggest?

Many teachers who endorse these aims and are anxious to liberate themselves and their students from an obsession with print and grades become frustrated when they try to work with movies. Generalities like "visual literacy" and "cinemacy" or "mediocracy" do not say enough about what to do with the class. Surely, teaching the grammar of film alone will ruin movies, yet film criticism is a sophisticated discipline which usually requires considerable exposure, a knowledge of film history, and experience with several critical viewpoints. What should a teacher know about media in order to help students grow, and how can he learn it efficiently? Must a movie teacher be a film buff? If the techniques for teaching movies are different from most teaching practices, how can a teacher learn them, and should he worry about behaving inconsistently—free and open one day, strict and structured the next?

These are exactly the kinds of questions this book addresses. Chapter 2, for instance, introduces the central technique for getting students and teachers to take their hearts as well as their heads to the movies; the technique is the basis for a variety of procedures designed to bring feelings into the classroom. Chapters 3 and 4 develop this technique in detail, showing a host of other related procedures that can be used to bring the bluebirds in the front row and the buzzards in the back into the same conversation. Some procedures indicate how movies can be used to bring science and math classes together with English or social studies classes, perhaps bringing coaches, English teachers, math teachers, and principals to the same lunch table. Another aim is to show how teachers can make movies live in the classroom by starting where they are right now. However, teaching with movies, though the major focus of this book, is not its sole topic. Equally important is what film study signifies about changing directions in education and how the teacher himself might promote change. This is the subject of the final two chapters, which are designed to offer support as well as challenge.

The importance of stimulating change is implicit throughout this book. One of the many attractions of using movies, in fact, is that through them a teacher may begin addressing from within the system the overwhelming problems that education faces. A host of educational Cassandras have been warning us that if we do not do something about redesigning educational strategies and systems, it will be too late—and time *is* running out. Buckminster Fuller maintains that we face either Utopia or oblivion, and that the forces of oblivion have the upper hand. Movies may be a countervailing force, however. For example:

Norbert Weiner[6] says that schools shield kids from reality. One of the most obvious realities, of course, is the mass media, which teachers proverbially abhor. Screen educators do not. Kids must learn about the mass media not only so they can cope with information overload, but also so they can respond to it imaginatively and use it expressively. Watching, discussing, and making movies provide this chance. At the same time, a teacher is in an enviable position to help students refine their abilities to perceive, to interpret, and eventually to judge.

John Gardner charges that schools promote obsolescence. The screen, though, will not become obsolete, since screen information is likely to increase rather than decrease. Exposure alone, naturally, will not solve problems; in fact, the major problem is overexposure, leading to desensitization. The teacher's task is to sensitize students, to help them discriminate so they will be able to adapt to rather than resist or merely conform to change. The teacher must help students to choose freely, for the free man cannot become obsolete.

Edgar Friedenberg[7] accuses the schools of punishing independence and creativity. By helping students discuss and make movies, though, we can encourage creativity and independence. As a student finds out how he sees and interprets what he sees, he can use this experience as a basis for further experience and further understanding. Discovering the particular ways we see and feel, and refining our individual ways of expressing ourselves, open us to many other possibilities for learning. And what is creativity but openness in action?

John Holt has shown that schools are places of fear and competition, a feeling that Knowles captured in *A Separate Peace,* which is one reason why students respond so well to that novel.

---

[6]Norbert Weiner, a scientist, is the father of cybernetics. His ideas have had a profound influence on our notions of man as a feedback organism. He is the author of *The Human Use of Human Beings. Cybernetics and Society.*

[7]Edgar Friedenberg is a critic of education best known for his work in psychology and sociology. His book *The Vanishing Adolescent* has heavily influenced recent thinking about the nature and purposes of high school education.

(Even at Devon, in that novel, a movie momentarily broke through the fear, when a ski patrol film prompted Leper to desert the school and join the service, only to desert that, too. Possibly a sensitive teacher could have used that propaganda film to help Leper recognize and deal constructively with his fear and frustration.) Teachers who use movies can begin to replace fear with fun; the fun becomes learning when the student begins to share his particular way of experiencing the film with others.

It is the quality of this sharing that determines whether the game-like atmosphere of such learning is constructive or destructive. It all depends on what the object of the game is. Games occur constantly in classrooms, but they are usually the destructive, selfish kind, the sort that feature put-downs or point-scoring in the version called "Guess what's on my mind?" The purpose of film study, on the other hand, is to play games in which, as Finny said about Blitzball, "everybody wins."

Finally, Carl Rogers[8] believes that schools do not promote personally significant learnings. He says that we need not static, codified answers, but "changing, process answers," and that the proper aim of education must be the facilitation of change and learning. His ideas about student-directed learning and his own technique of facilitating classes with basic encounter groups are major and growing contributions to humanistic education.

Movies fit Rogers" views beautifully. By evoking feelings in the classroom, they set the stage for people to begin sharing what they care about. Each student becomes a critic, but as he shares his experiences with others he illuminates and often alters his own views. Answers in a film class must always reflect change and process because they emerge from encounters between people rather than from ideas alone. In a film class the teacher also is a learner who must constantly revise his own answers as he learns not only to listen to his students but to *hear* them.

Robert Frost once said that nothing scared him more than scared people. Similarly, nothing should scare screen educators more than scared colleagues, administrators, and parents. Teachers fear a new medium because it threatens their position and role, it consumes time, and students sometimes like it more than they do the teacher. Administrators fear it because it costs money,

---

[8]Carl Rogers is a psychologist whose development of client-centered therapy has also led to analogous approaches to education. Two of his best-known books that are particularly useful for teachers are *On Becoming a Person* and *Freedom To Learn* (see Appendix II).

takes time, and is different. Parents fear it too, because it doesn't seem to have much to do with "school." Certainly, movies provoke these and other fears largely because they so dramatically challenge conventional notions of schooling. The challenge to screen educators is to dispel fear in their own classes and to invite others to reap the benefits as well, and further, to begin changing the values that people normally associate with school. As for parents and administrators, don't avoid them—educate them.

2

WHAT TO DO WHEN THE LIGHTS GO ON?

We can't reduce a film experience to a few neat lessons. Audiences see movies in vastly different ways, and no package of discrete concepts or interpretations can encompass all those ways of experiencing. Although this may be true with any form of art, the students' emotional investments in an intense film experience make it especially difficult for anyone to get by with conventional approaches. If he tries, students either will resist or will merely play along and fail to grow.

In order to take advantage of the immediacy and richness of the film experience, the teacher must teach inductively, but he must use techniques different from most inductive approaches that work with literature and social studies.

COMMUNICATION

Film does not communicate in the same way printed literature does, despite its superficial resemblance to drama and fiction. Even the documentary, which resembles the essay, does not communicate in the same way as a magazine article or newspaper story. Films communicate by images and sounds organized around elements of composition, rhythm, tempo, pace, lighting, color, music, and symbols. The interaction of these elements in movies, calling on both thought and feeling, is the essence of the film-maker's art.

We cannot teach movies by using the techniques that succeed in other subjects, then, because movies are special types of experiences with their own forms, language, and kinds of meaning. When movies are taught deductively or as if they were literature, the sense of interaction — of art — is lost in translation. Ingmar Bergman said bluntly that film has nothing to do with literature; Suzanne Langer,[1] searching for the most appropriate comparison

---

[1] Suzanne Langer is a philosopher specializing in aesthetic theory. Her comments on film appear in *Feeling and Form*. (New York: Charles Scribner's Sons, 1953, pp. 411-415.)

with other genres, came up with the idea that film is the "mode of dream."

ENTERTAINMENT, QUALITY, AND EDUCATION

These observations present special problems for teachers interested in using movies, primarily because they may select movies according to limited criteria, and may teach accordingly. Arthur Knight, in his excellent history of the movies *The Liveliest Art*,[2] tells a story that carries a lesson for today's schools and teachers. Most movies in the nickelodeon era, such as the one-reel westerns, pretended to be nothing more than entertainment. In 1907, however, a French company called Film d'Art attempted to introduce the mass film audience to the greatest artists in the French repertory theater. Using the most remarkable talents available, the company quickly developed a wide range of classic theatrical productions in their mission of bringing culture to the Great Unwashed. The masses, to their credit, stayed away from the films, but the "right people" attended and brought prestige to the movies. Producers from other countries presented Dickens, Shakespeare (*Hamlet*, silent and frantic, in 10 minutes), and a variety of other classics. Ironically, these clumsy "art" films were inferior to the primitive *Great Train Robbery*, an important early contribution to the artistic growth of American movies.

The difference in quality, then, involved a distinction that still gives trouble to contemporary viewers, especially teachers who want to use film for educational purposes. The problem with the "art" films is that they ignore the elements mentioned above, the essential ingredients of communication in film. The problem is not with the raw material of the films, for surely all good drama or ballet entertains. Rather, the problem comes when entertainment becomes culturally pretentious or sententious, and ignores characteristics of the medium. That is the difference between "art" movies and great, entertaining movies, and it is as important a difference for today's educators to consider as it was for audiences during the infancy of American movies.

This historical note underlines how from the very beginning American movies have had to work within the entertainment form; cultural prestige has often been misguided. The artificial distinc-

---

[2]See Appendix I for a listing of books on film and film study.

Figure 1. Dream of the Wild Horses.
Courtesy Pathe-Contemporary Films/McGraw-Hill

tion between the popular movie and the art house movie still plagues the industry itself, and it is egregiously evident in schools. Ordinarily, schools are much more willing to order a filmed Shakespearean play than a John Ford western, simply because they are still accustomed to believing that literature or "enriching" artistic productions are intrinsically more educational than any western could possibly be. Shakespeare can be superb on film (*Henry V* seems made for the movies, and the film is excellent), but the film *Henry V* may be selected primarily because it is Shakespearean; its qualities as film become purely serendipitous.

As a result, well-meaning traditional educators may pay attention to the wrong elements in movies. Like the audiences of 1907, they may be more concerned with the subject matter of a movie than with its art. The problem a teacher faces, then, is how to reconcile a nonrational, present-oriented genre with the scholastic

13

Figure 2. Dream of the Wild Horses.
Courtesy Pathe-Contemporary Films/McGraw-Hill

tradition of rational analysis. How can he avoid making movies fit a Procrustean bed?

One way is to avoid forced evaluation. We tend to assume that students should evaluate any work they study, especially since they tend to judge movies anyhow, using vague or purely visceral criteria. The highly subjective nature of the film art—and the growing awareness among audiences of the personal influence of the director upon a movie—further invites evaluation. If we wish students to develop their own standards of judgment, though, we should wait for standards to grow. And they will, gradually, emerge from a variety of viewpoints about a shared experience and increasingly careful examination of the factors contributing to that experience. This examination, rather than evaluation, should be the focus for classroom activities.

We can avoid evaluation by not setting rigid guidelines about what, when, why, and how to teach specific films. Instead we should explore the individual aesthetic of each film in order to remain flexible and inductive. Considering the tremendous range of forms that movies have assumed and continue to assume, this tentativeness is essential. It seems that the teacher, with his class, must examine each concrete film experience itself rather than general statements about a film or about films as a genre.

The film movement has gained enough momentum for many schools to be well aware of the short and feature films available, and the number of books and articles about film study is growing steadily. In searching for reliable, familiar approaches to using movies in schools, it is tempting to tighten things up, to set clear but rigid guidelines. As a result, some of the most popular films

Figure 3.   *The Hand.*

Courtesy Pathe-Contemporary Films/McGraw-Hill

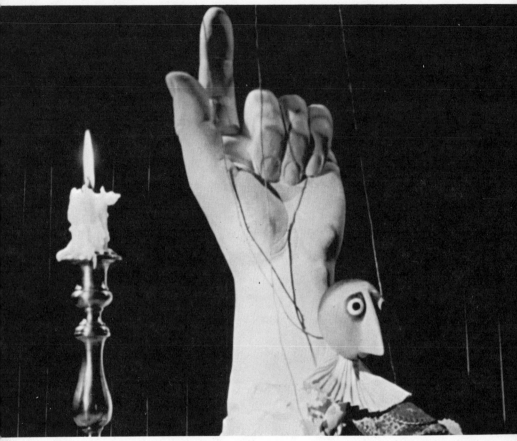

Figure 4. The Hand.
Courtesy Pathe-Contemporary Films/McGraw-Hill

like *Dream of the Wild Horses, Neighbors, Toys,* and *David and Lisa* may become as entrenched in schools as *A Separate Peace* and "The Road Not Taken." Soon Cliff and Monarch may discover a great new market in film trots.[3]

John Culkin has said that movies are valuable because they have "zap"—that which turns kids on. No one wants to stifle zap, of course, but conditioned by long devotion to verbal disciplines, we nurture precision and generalization and consequently cop out on the problem of what to talk about after the lights go on. As a result, we commonly follow the rule that "I saw" is less important than "I think."

----

[3]See Appendix IV for the distributors of most of the films mentioned in the text. See Appendix V for addresses of film distributors.

Students are no more liberated from this rule than teachers are. At one film conference, for instance, I overheard this conversation between two juniors:

"What did *The Hand* symbolize?"
"Forces against bad things—you know, commies and stuff."
"Yeah, that's what I thought."

They were serious, almost grave. Not a hint of sarcasm, no comment that either of them found the film pretentious, contrived, scary, boring, or involving. They sought labels.

THE OLD SCHOOL GAME

Conduct or observe a free discussion or examine a batch of free-topic papers on a movie and you'll find that students are often playing the old school game of telling Teacher what they think He wants to hear, or talking or writing about "hidden meanings" or "true significance," rather than truly experiencing the film itself.

Unquestionably, movies can reinforce the school game by helping more kids play it successfully. As teachers testify, a film often stimulates the buzzard in the back row to explore complex ideas. A case in point: After a class of nonacademic inner city students had discussed *Dream of the Wild Horses,* everyone agreed that the discussion had been the best all year. That is, students had been interested and frequently excited, and they had contributed thoughtful generalizations supported with evidence from the film. As one teacher proudly stated, "If you didn't know, you'd never guess they were nonacademic kids."

One student's comment after class, however, revealed another view:

"I loved the movie," she said, "but I didn't get it."
"What do you mean?"
"I didn't get what it meant. Especially the fire part."
"Why did it have to mean something?" I asked.
Then she grinned—surely I was putting her on (and maybe I was, at that!). "Well, you know—well, it's *got* to mean something."

Just because nonacademic kids are beginning to sound learned is not necessarily cause to celebrate. Relieved of the burden of print, mediocre students often demonstrate that they, too, can play Deep Inner Meanings. Many interpretations, however fervently defended, are little more than exercises in cleverness. Granted, someone may truly consider a film to be "a visual poem about conformity," but he shouldn't feel obligated to mine gems like that.

Kids should react directly to a movie; that is, they should react with feelings as well as thoughts to get the most out of the experience. Moreover, if they feel *compelled* to intellectualize about the movie, they will miss the experience. There is no point in seeing a film if you intend to treat it like a poem, since then you might just as well read a poem. Even though there may be some reason for the teacher to get excited about the intellectual awakening of nonacademic kids, he is settling for less than what is possible.

For this reason, I sometimes think the most disarmingly valuable film around is *The Critic*, a delightful five-minute spoof of a boorish, self-appointed critic who reads meanings into an abstract film. "I paid two bucks to see dis?" he grumbles. "Dis is a film about da sex life of two things."

One of the most effective ways to use this film, incidentally, is to show it first without the sound and invite comments. Invariably some students come up with ingenious interpretations and theories. When they view the film with its soundtrack, they experience a true shock of recognition. This exercise is all in fun, of course, but it can help focus attention on the dangers of ingenuity. The class can then discuss when ingenious interpretations legitimately apply.

MEANINGS FOR WHOM?

Discussions of Deep Inner Meanings may be inevitable, and if students are excited by the lively talk they should not be discouraged from it. Lively, intelligent talk is rare enough, especially in the classroom. But if a student is to find his own meaning in a film, he should not feel coerced by teachers, other students, or the environment itself into thinking that meaning is intellectual content. The verbally adept or aggressive student may dictate the thinking of those who want to contribute but aren't quite sure how to begin. As a result, visceral reactions aren't considered legitimate in discussion:

"Fantastic movie!"
"Define your terms."

Figure 5. Clay.
Courtesy Pathe-Contemporary Films/McGraw-Hill

The problem with an interchange like that is not simply that the teacher is insensitive and pedantic, but that even if he weren't so stuffy the conversation might still center upon evaluation. Surely it is important to ask the student to define what he means, but it is even more important to examine how the "fantastic" movie communicated. In fact, the student might discover that "fantastic" is the best word he could have found, but not for the reasons he used it. To translate "fantastic" either into a more academically acceptable judgment of the film or to reduce the experience to literary terms is to ignore the uniqueness of a specific aesthetic experience.

An obvious example of the problem is *Clay* (see Figs. 5 and 6), which Putsch describes as "an amusing and experimental reca-

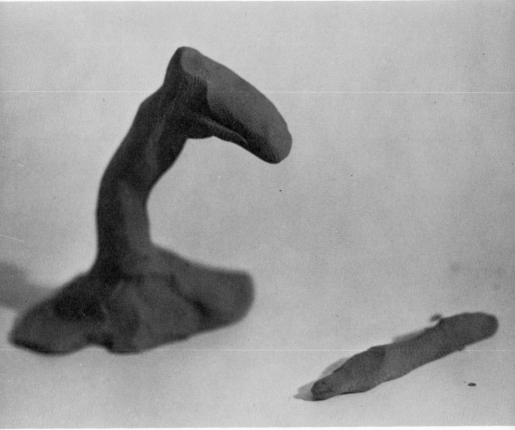

Figure 6. Clay.

Courtesy Pathe-Contemporary Films/McGraw-Hill

pitulation of Darwin's *The Origin of Species* in animated clay."[4] There is a surprise ending, though, when a monster devours the Statue of Liberty. A teacher could use this image as a basis for discussion of Social Darwinism or forces threatening freedom. In fact, a student may raise the issue and release the teacher from any charge of imposing a hidden agenda. However, as any four-year-old can tell you, the appeal of *Clay* has nothing to do with that issue. The appeal is in watching those delightful things wiggle, grow, sniff, jump, skate, sprout, bite, and gobble in time to a jazzy soundtrack. And if you missed the import of the ending, so what?

The problem is tricky, though, for if a student says he finds his own meaning in the social implications of the final image (else

[4]Mallery, D.: *Film in the Life of the School.* Boston: National Association of Independent Schools, 1968, p. 39.

why is it there?), then what right has anyone to impose an anti-intellectual interpretation? By the same token, a teacher or student may impose an intellectual interpretation by automatically pursuing theme because it is conventional classroom fodder and because the images themselves resist discussion. The difficulty is widespread, for a great many visually exciting films are also somewhat didactic—*Glass; Neighbors; Rhinoceros; Very Nice, Very Nice;* and *Toys,* for example. Many of those which are not overtly didactic—*Corral, Leaf,* and *Dream of the Wild Horses,* for instance—invite didactic interpretations.

The paraphrasable content of a short film, almost tailored for classroom use, tempts us to make a film earn its keep with verbal dividends. After all, we've barely been able to immerse ourselves in a short film when we're back in the classroom and it's time to

Figure 7. Time Piece.
Courtesy Pathe-Contemporary Films/McGraw-Hill

do something constructive. Many times, students who want to prolong the experience suggest a simple and by no means trivial solution:

"Play it again, Sam!"
"Again? And waste valuable class discussion time?"

Many films are shown because they fit units in English, social studies, and humanities courses. These films are not mere audio-visual aids to printed matter; they are valuable experiences in themselves. Nevertheless, their use in specific units reinforces the impression that generalizations matter most. Even strikingly experimental films like *Run!; Very Nice, Very Nice;* and *Time Piece* can become as pat as lectures, for the fast cuts and clever montages satirize the absurd urban rat race as surely as goats mean sex.

Figure 8. *Time Piece.*
Courtesy Pathe-Contemporary Films/McGraw-Hill

Figure 9. *Time Piece.*
Courtesy Pathe-Contemporary Films/McGraw-Hill

Jean Paul Sartre said, "The greatest sin is to turn what is concrete into an abstraction"; it is difficult to resist this temptation in film study. At a recent showing of short films, I saw *Orange,* a sensual three minutes of a mouth eating an orange. The audience cheered, but the program notes were more restrained: "A sensual lesson in the absurdity of objects," they said. Whether the orange is an absurd object, I don't know, but I object particularly to the word "lesson." It is as if the sensual experience were not valuable in and of itself but instead had to be translated into a message. Perhaps the writer was on the spot—he had to write something under pressing circumstances. It struck me, however, that his situation must have closely resembled the pressure on a student to say something bright when the lights go on.

Curriculum planners and teachers unintentionally encourage such transgressions. Naturally, English, social studies, and humanities courses neglect purely aesthetic concerns in favor of theme. If a film is part of a regular unit (perhaps war, or the individual's role in society), it is difficult for a student to enjoy the film solely for whatever personal resonances or visual excitement he may find in it. There is bound to be a Deep Inner Meaning, and he must ferret it out. In addition, some filmmakers have "meanings" that they wish to convey; McLaren, for example, in *Neighbors*. The search is not necessarily a chore, either, for as we know, movies can make learning fun.

We are not so naive that we equate meaning with paraphrase. Since content in film, as in any art, emerges from the details of style, we ask for specific evidence to support generalizations just as we would if we were teaching literature. It's hard, though, to talk about meaning, even supporting generalizations with specifics, because we tend to forget specifics fairly quickly. As a result we often sacrifice full aesthetic involvement for lively discussion and call it a fair trade.

However, a free and loose discussion to promote new understandings as a result of deep aesthetic experience does require a lot of specific reaction and interaction. Because this is frustrating and sometimes impossible if we lose touch with specifics, we should spend a great deal of time sharing concrete observations, expanding the richness and variety of perceptions, delaying interpretation and criticism, and above all reserving judgment.

Insightful criticism depends upon how deeply and richly the critic sees. A class untrained to perceive details of composition like color, setting, and rhythm probably won't generate sensitive criticism because it will have lost touch with the concrete experience it is supposedly discussing.

THE IMAGE-SOUND SKIM

A technique to help the students stay in touch with the specifics is needed to maintain a rich discussion. The most valuable device I have found in sharing what we see is the image-sound skim, a procedure commonly used to open discussion after a film, but rarely extended beyond that point. To conduct an image-sound skim, a teacher asks each student to mention some images or sounds from the film which spring immediately to mind. The device loosens kids up by giving everybody a chance to talk without fear of being wrong, and to encourage them to think in terms of the film itself. However, the procedure can be extended so that it becomes the content of the entire discussion. As images and sounds are recalled, they prompt other images and sounds by association, and students being to reorchestrate the movie in the present and learn how others in the class perceive. It is easy to avoid straying from the film itself, and everyone accumulates a great deal of concrete material for a truly inductive expansion of the implications arising out of the session.

In this type of class, not only is there no premium on agreement with a moderator or whiz kid (there isn't anything to agree with, most of the time, except whether an image or sound actually did occur); it is not even necessary to reach conclusions. What emerges instead is a gradually richer set of relationships among images, sounds, and implied ideas. In this way, the art of the film, instead of being killed by excessive analysis, has a fair chance to continue working on the audience. Rhythms, details of setting, mood, counterpoints, transitions, color, and lighting subtly affect the processes by which students recall images and sounds.

This is the central technique for avoiding the search for Deep Inner Meanings, labels, and arbitrary judgments. It is designed to provide a way to approach a film from within, to examine the structure of an individual film while sticking to the cinematic experience itself. Because all other techniques mentioned in the following pages grow from or are consistent with this basic reasoning, they can be used to complement each other. The next two chapters discuss in detail how to use the image-sound skim as well as many other related techniques, what kinds of questions to ask, and the teacher's role in keeping the experience growing.

Although there are many ways to use movies in classrooms, the main purpose is to enlarge the emotional and intellectual territory in which a student perceives himself. Thus, "good" discussion of general ideas is not an end in itself. What matters most is the sensibility—the perceptions upon which verbalizations are based.

The procedures I describe in the following chapters, then, are designed on the premise that in order to sensitize students to the medium of film and to make them more open to one another, we must discover how and what each other sees. From these procedures may emerge what Ron Sutton has called "a kind of vocabulary that we can share when we are talking about some things that really matter. An image here, a line or design there, a recurring piece of dialogue, a reminder of audience response or discussion—these become a kind of currency of communication."[5]

[5]Ron Sutton, formerly Education Director of the American Film Institute, is now with the Center for Understanding Media, in New York City. Quoted in Mallery, D.: *Film in the Life of the School.* Boston: National Association of Independent Schools, 1968, p. 5.

3

IMAGE-SOUND SKIMMING: IN-SIGHT

This chapter and the next describe the image-sound skim and a body of related classroom procedures. However, these techniques may become mere cookbook approaches unless they are used systematically. I have seen many classes where teachers have used these techniques without carefully considering *why* they were using them, other than that they had seen them work elsewhere, or had heard about them. Even though some of these classes were "good" in conventional terms, they fell far short of what they might have been.

Subsequent discussions with teachers showed invariably that they had not thought carefully about the *process* objectives of the techniques. They were concerned about reaching familiar subject matter objectives and stimulating lively discussion, and because they were accomplishing both to some extent they had no complaints. Neither do I, on one level; there is nothing wrong with accomplishing what you set out to do. It is possible, though, to generate much more liveliness and substance from film study than we usually believe we can.

The image-sound skim is the basis of a collaborative approach to systematically integrating feelings and intuition with intellectual concerns. The ways in which academic and art courses usually segregate feelings and intellect are often reflected in film study programs, especially during the early stages. Because film study tends to become tailored to conventional objectives often based upon arbitrary notions of what students ought to know, or isolated as a peripheral art course, or treated as a refreshing and fruitful interlude among more essential units of study, it often fails to correspond to the ways students actually grow and develop mentally and personally.

This difficulty is almost inevitable because movies generally enter schools on the coattails of other established subjects, and most procedures for teaching movies have been based on the goals of these subjects. In order to offset the effects of the typical academic method of film study, screen educators have devised a number of other approaches to teaching with film. Unfortunately, these approaches are not closely related. The major trends are to treat film as art, or as an important environmental and cultural factor, or as a special language—what Paul Carrico[1] has called "the distinctive idiom of the twentieth century."

The study of film as art emphasizes how film, composed of many arts, is a separate, unique, and autonomous art form. Paying close attention to film history and examining elements of film such as rhythm, color, composition, and techniques of editing and camerawork, this approach usually features analysis and evaluation of outstanding films.

A contrasting approach, derived largely from McLuhan's ideas, pays scant attention to content, form, or structure of film and concentrates instead on how the medium has affected our society and our habits of perception. This approach gives equal time to the impact of other mass media, especially television. A related approach involves studying movies from a sociological standpoint; that is, studying how movies have reflected or commented upon various forces in the society.

The study of the elements and language of film, the third major approach, has recently begun to avoid evaluation of film on the assumption or hope that more perceptive students will become more aesthetically sensitive and will generate their own valid criteria for judging films. This approach often stresses student filmmaking, and fortunately a number of lucid, detailed articles and books on student filmmaking have been written to nurture it through its infancy (see Appendix I).

Despite strong biases, most screen educators agree that no one approach is the "right" one, and consequently they settle upon a flexible combination of approaches. Each teacher, of course, will probably select whatever combination of approaches he feels most comfortable with. Because film study is still so new, however, he may select or combine approaches arbitrarily, he may experiment haphazardly, or he may become disappointed by uneven results and conclude that movies are simply another bright bottle for the same old wine. The image-sound skim, however, buttressed by a clear rationale, may serve to help.

---

[1]Paul Carrico developed film courses at Notre Dame High School for Boys in Niles, Illinois. He also founded the Screen Educators Society in Chicago, and the film magazine *See*.

GENERAL THEORY

The general theory behind the image-sound skim, drawn largely from Jean Piaget, Jerome Bruner,[2] and Carl Rogers, holds that an individual learner "knows" at any moment what he needs to know and can learn, and that in a supportive environment he will pursue his own learning energetically. "Energetic learning" is actually a tautology, for purely receptive mental activity does not exist, and what we mean by development and growth is the activity of selecting, processing, and transforming information. The major obstacle to the child's learning is his tendency to adhere to limited viewpoints determined by his situation in time and space, and his emotional history. For this reason, discussion of movies should concentrate on fresh, shifting points of view and on the *activity* of seeing.

TECHNIQUES

Just as a group must not restrict itself arbitrarily to one or two interpretations of a movie, neither should it embrace only one or two approaches to studying a movie. The group, together with the teacher, must explore many avenues, sometimes more than once, if it is to become aware of the process involved in fully experiencing a film. Becoming aware of this process, rather than learning a particular fact or concept, should be a central aim of film study.

In light of this rationale, film education should reflect as much as possible a collaborative design of a mechanism by which the students and the teacher can accommodate whatever approaches they find most effective at the time. This design must be flexible and can include the history and critical analysis of films, and the use of film to supplement other activities. There is no fixed rule on teaching procedures, either, for these must fit emerging objectives and the individual style of the teacher.

Using this rationale, a teacher may experiment with some clear general objectives in mind. These objectives will not be the usual ones of the academic curriculum, nor will they belong solely in the artist's domain. Instead, they will be designed to encourage exploration of ideas, analysis, intellectual synthesis, expression and interpretation of feeling, self-examination, the study or discussion of actual classroom behavior in relation to the film, and

---

[2]Jerome Bruner, a psychologist, has specialized in cognitive development. His best-known work in education is *The Process of Education*. He teaches at Oxford University in England.

creative expression through student filmmaking, without necessarily prescribing priorities to any one of these activities.

The objectives of the class are not selected willy-nilly purely on the basis of whim or the feeling in the classroom at the time, but with predetermined ends that have been set as much as possible through negotiation with the class, a method that helps in selecting different goals at different times. The feeling in the classroom must be considered, since a flagging discussion or other activity is not likely to reach desired ends. Frequently the teacher may have the best suggestion for a way to continue, but if the class achieves consensus about it, the entire group is more likely to participate actively in making the method work. Before the group can arrive at any consensus, however, it must generate data to work from; the image-sound skim is ideally suited to this purpose.

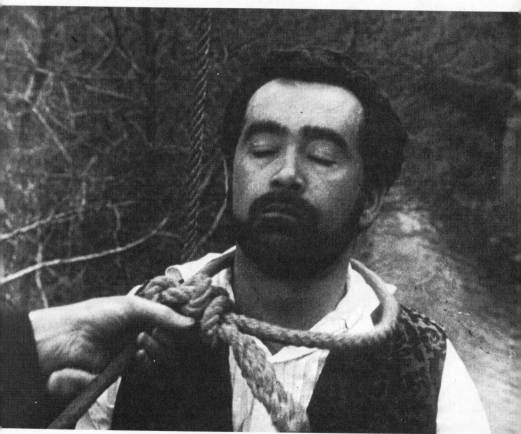

Figure 10. An Occurrence at Owl Creek Bridge.
Courtesy Pathe-Contemporary Films/McGraw-Hill

As this brief theoretical background indicates, the image-sound skim, the body of related procedures described in the next chapter, and other experimental devices that might grow from this approach will be no more than a bag of tricks unless there is a spirit of collaborative design in film study. This spirit depends upon the degree to which the teacher can change his behavior toward facilitation.

Facilitating image-sound skimming is designed to build a bridge between feeling and thought; that is, between intuitive, often visceral, reactions and intellectual appraisals. Image-sound skimming is an inventory of the content of the various levels on which we see the film. On one level we may simply catalogue prominent images — usually what the director has emphasized. On another level we may examine feelings about the images; on a third level we may investigate a variety of other associations; and finally we may discuss ideas that the images suggest.

We can see how this process operates by examining one of the best-known shorts that has been shown frequently on television as well as in schools across the country: Robert Enrico's *An Occurrence at Owl Creek Bridge*, an adaptation of Ambrose Bierce's short story. (See Figs. 10, 11, and 12.) It is about a man's fantasies during the moments just prior to his execution. It won the Cannes Film Festival prize, and is widely considered to be one of the most beautiful and powerful short films available.

In this film, as Peyton Farquhar is standing on the end of a plank jutting from the side of the bridge, the noose around his neck, he shuts his eyes and momentarily thinks of his wife and home (see Fig. 10). Moments later, as a soldier releases the plank, he plunges toward the water below. The rope suddenly breaks. In the water, Farquhar extricates himself from his ropes, struggles to the surface, and gasps for air. Soldiers shoot at him, but he escapes by swimming downstream, through rapids, to a sandy beach. During the rest of the film he eludes the soldiers, runs through the woods and down a road, and finally arrives home, runs to his wife, then suddenly jerks convulsively. We discover that his escape was merely a brief fantasy — he had been hanged.

At the point where he surfaces in the water, there begins a long sequence in which we see his face as he gazes around him. (See Fig. 11 sequence.) The camera turns to the trees above him, and we hear a song about the joy of life — "A Livin' Man," — during which we see a series of slow-motion shots that record details of life around him: a caterpillar on a leaf, a spider weaving a delicate web. The details are a visual counterpart to the song's affirmation.

(Text continued on page 36.)

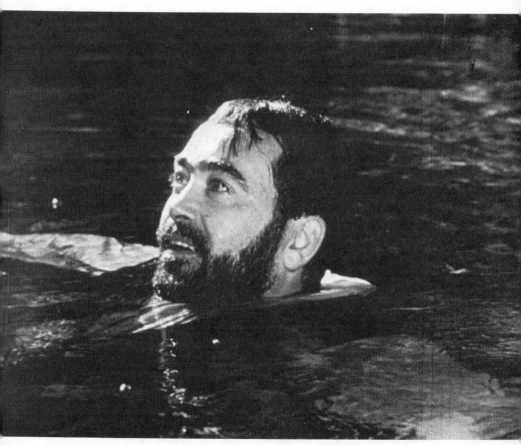

Figure 11A. An Occurrence at Owl Creek Bridge.

Courtesy Pathe-Contemporary Films/McGraw-Hill

Figure 11B.   An Occurrence at Owl Creek Bridge.

Courtesy Pathe-Contemporary Films/McGraw-Hill

Figure 11C. An Occurrence at Owl Creek Bridge.

Courtesy Pathe-Contemporary Films/McGraw-Hill

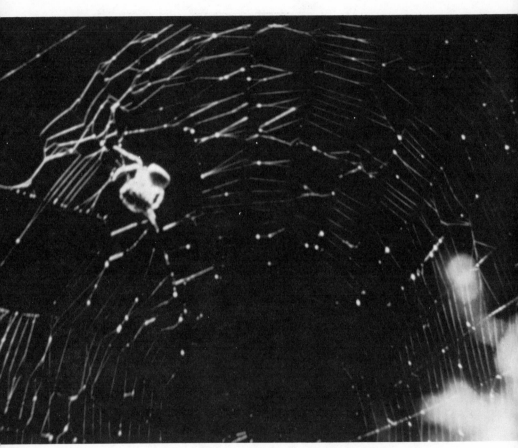

Figure 11D. An Occurrence at Owl Creek Bridge.

Courtesy Pathe-Contemporary Films/McGraw-Hill

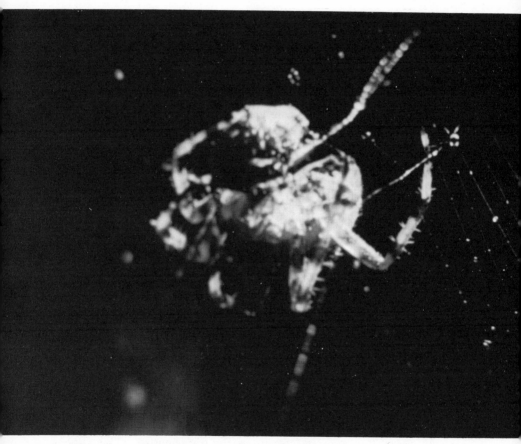

Figure 11E. An Occurrence at Owl Creek Bridge.

Courtesy Pathe-Contemporary Films/McGraw-Hill

Among these details, the image of the spider invites the following interpretation, which might emerge from the skimming exercise: Moments after the image of the spider, Farquhar again becomes aware of the soldiers. They are preparing to shoot him in the water, and a voice shouts that he is "in a trap." The spider image, therefore, acquires additional significance. While it is beautiful and delicate, it is also menacing. As we first see it, however, we are paying attention to the song and the images of life; like Farquhar, we are momentarily unaware of threats. The spider image therefore evokes negative feelings that prepare us for the return to the problem of escaping, but without the image-sound skim we remain unaware of the subtle effect of the juxtaposition. In fact, the shot works because it creates dissonance between image and sound.

Initially, the spider appears simply to be one of several visual counterparts to the song. Although the song does not mention a spider, it does mention a butterfly, and in any case the sequence is visually explicit; the spider does not appear to be a symbol. First we see a shot of the man's face as he looks intensely and gladly around him, and then we see the details themselves. However, the man cannot possibly see the intricately detailed close-ups that we see. The scene represents an attitude toward experience rather than exactly what Farquhar sees. Thus, Enrico is using the images in several different ways to achieve different purposes, many of which depend on the audience's visceral reactions to a spider. It is such intuitively felt details that collectively create the total artistic effect of a film.

Sergei Eisenstein (see Appendix I) stated the principle long ago, that shot A plus shot B is more than the sum of A plus B. Thus, the simple sequence of shots is a filmic "idea": the shot of the man's face plus the shot of an insect on a leaf implies that the man is looking at the insect. However, the way in which the sequence is presented, the context of the shot, our feelings about the details and the content, and our feelings about the man himself affect the way we organize the information. The process creates dimensions of experience and knowledge that resist logical, linear analysis but yield to the less restrictive climate of the image-sound skim.

One could successfully defend another, opposite interpretation of the spider image. Although the spider typically carries a strongly negative association, this sequence reverses them. The spider is usually a symbol of death; here it is a symbol of life. In this moment of intense awareness of the preciousness of life, even the spider brings wonder and joy.

Figure 12. *An Occurrence at Owl Creek Bridge.*
Courtesy Pathe-Contemporary Films/McGraw-Hill

Ultimately the "correct" interpretation of this sequence must be subjective. What is most important for the class is not to arrive at an unequivocal conclusion about this issue but to become aware of the feelings and suggestions surrounding the images and sounds. The critical distinction which may follow then becomes another matter—important, but not most essential.

This exercise helps students to perceive more richly, and helps the teacher to concentrate on the way the members of the audience, including himself, are thinking, feeling, and seeing—that is, perceiving. The actual procedure of the exercise may take a variety of forms. A group may simply catalogue images and sounds for a specified time, then discuss them, but usually discussion emerges spontaneously.

A hypothetical discussion with high school students follows. In this session, students have been recalling images and sounds without further comment. They have been trying to get in touch with the experience they've just had, and have been talking for about four or five minutes.

John: Butterfly.

Mary: You mean in the song.

John: No, not then. It was when he was on the beach, grabbing the sand. There was this butterfly that flew into the screen on the left near the bottom.

Peter: I don't remember any butterfly.

John: Just for a second.

Joanne: I noticed it too, I think. Something. Like it wasn't important, though. It just went by. I mean, he didn't make a big deal about it.

John: Yeah.

Alice: Speaking of bugs — ick!

Linda: Oh, Alice, they weren't that bad.

Alice: I suppose you'd say they were cute.

Teacher: Did *he* think they were — how did he see them?

Peter: He liked them, I guess.

Teacher: You guess.

Peter: He was still alive.

Teacher: What do you mean?

Peter: Well, you know. He was just glad he was alive.

Linda: He rolls around in the sand.

George: But that was later. Right then he was just looking around.

Alice: At the bugs. No, really. I mean, actually he liked them. It was the way he looked at them. Maybe he didn't, usually, I don't know. But just then he was glad to see anything.

John: The song, too.

Linda: Yeah. It said he was turned on to everything.

Peter: Because he was alive.

Alice: Anyway, he felt different about the bugs than I did.

Teacher: George?

George: I thought it was stupid. Boring. And too much, that faggy bit about smelling the flower.

Linda:	That was later.
John:	Yeah. On the beach. When the butterfly went by.
Alice:	I don't see how you saw that butterfly. I want to see it again to check.
John:	You're just scared of bugs, that's all.
Alice:	Spiders, yes. Butterflies are fine.
John:	Look, the whole butterfly thing is a pure accident anyway. A fluke.
Peter:	Hey, I don't see why we're spending so much time on this. What's the point? He said it was just a fluke.
Linda:	I don't know. Maybe not. Maybe they wanted the butterfly in. I mean, you don't actually *know* it was an accident.
John:	Don't worry, I know.
Joanne:	Will somebody please tell me what's going on in here? What are you *talking* about?
Teacher:	Does it matter whether we could prove that Enrico used that shot of the butterfly deliberately? How would you go about proving it?
John:	Hardly anybody noticed it. It's just something I saw. Part of the scenery was all.
Bob:	It's only important if the camera pointed it out, right?
Peter:	Most people don't notice it. Only nature freaks like John.
Teacher:	Why do you suppose Enrico spent so much time on the scene with the song? Why doesn't he get on with the story? Bob?
Bob:	That's the whole point of the movie. We don't notice anything until we nearly lose it. The time he was most alive was the second before he died. Like in Hemingway's story, *The Short Happy Life of Francis Macomber*.
Oscar:	Chalk up another "A" for Bobby-baby.
Teacher:	Okay, but let's wait on that idea for a while and get more images on the table. Any other images, someone?

This conversation is rich in possibilities; some are partially realized, some might be handled more effectively and some are lost. The discussion leader is more of a moderator and teacher than a facilitator, though the low proportion of teacher-talk is atypical and generally a step in the right direction. However, the students often seem not to be listening carefully to one another, and the teacher does not pick up the points they neglect. At one point the teacher cannot resist butting in to play straight man for Bob. Even though his question is related to ideas brought up in the discussion, the group is on a slightly different point at the time, and the question is obviously phrased to elicit an answer he has in mind—a "right" answer.

Perhaps if the leader resisted that tendency to "teach," Bob would not confine his comments to bright academic observations. Although the class is generally comfortable with the teacher, there may be more feeling behind Oscar's sarcastic comment than the teacher realizes. He might have developed possibilities by probing Alice's feelings about bugs, and he misses a great chance to capitalize on George's remark that smelling a flower was "faggy." Finally, by asking a leading question about theme and then postponing discussion of it in order to return to the exercise, he gives the class double signals. On the one hand he wants free, open discussion and recollection; on the other hand, he cannot resist a ready-made lesson plan, and he encourages other priorities.

If he tried facilitating, he would abandon playing the game of Guess-what's-on-my-mind and would respond to feelings more directly. Most important, he would offer more of himself. For instance, his discussion with the same group might contain exchanges like these:

Alice:	Speaking of bugs—ick!
Linda:	Oh, Alice, they weren't that bad.
Facilitator:	Did you feel "ick!" when you saw them in the film, or just about bugs in general?
Alice:	In general? Everytime I see a bug, especially a spider, forget it. One time I stood up on a chair for 10 minutes while this—spider!—crawled all around it.
Peter:	Probably more like 10 seconds.
Facilitator:	You don't mind spiders, Peter?
Peter:	I can do without them. but I don't climb the walls.
Facilitator:	Did you feel like climbing the walls when you saw the spider in the film, Alice?
Alice:	I sure did!

Linda: Oh, Alice, you did not.

Facilitator: I don't know how you feel, Alice, or how you really reacted to the spider image. Some people actually do feel as strongly as you say you do, but the way you're saying it make me wonder.

Alice: Well, I wasn't really scared, but I hate spiders.

Facilitator: How did you feel about *that* spider?

Alice: It was pretty, but still. . . .

Facilitator: You still had mixed feelings?

Alice: Yes. Well, I knew it was beautiful and all but . . . I don't know. I just hate spiders.

Facilitator: You say you *knew* it was beautiful.

Alice: It was supposed to be. He thought it was, the guy in the water, I mean.

Facilitator: How did the film show that?

Alice: The way he looked, and the song.

Peter: And the camerawork. Sort of like those Disney nature flicks. The wonderful world of bugs.

Alice: Ick.

Facilitator: But still you had mixed feelings about it. Anyone else have mixed feelings about that spider, or was it pure Disney?

In this exchange, the facilitator is still interested in the way the camera conveys ideas, but he is equally concerned with feelings. Alice's feelings about the spider may provide important information about the structure of the film, but the facilitator must obtain a precise statement of her feelings in order to help students to build on the implications, to compare their own reactions to hers. For this reason, he stops for a moment to examine process: how she is behaving.

In another situation he might examine process in greater detail, using a reaction to the film as a basis for developing insight into actual behavior. The following hypothetical exchange represents one way a student's reaction could lead to examining social norms acting in the classroom.

George: I thought it was stupid. Boring. And too much, that faggy bit about smelling the flower.

Linda: That was later.

Facilitator: George, you said a lot just then. Let's look at it. I'm a little bothered about that scene, too, but I don't know if it's for the same reason. You felt uncomfortable?

George: Yeah, a little. I don't really mean he's gay or anything. It just seemed too much, the way he did it.

Facilitator: Can you remember exactly when you started feeling uncomfortable? What was on the screen?

George: Right after he finished throwing the sand up in the air and looking around.

Facilitator: Can you put your finger on what bothered you then?

George: Well, there was a dead spot in there. I thought maybe he'd spot a soldier and have to fight him— I didn't know what would happen, really. And then there was this big flower sticking up in the screen and I just knew he was going to go ape over it. No way he could avoid it—no way.

Facilitator: It was a set-up?

George: Yeah. They'd already made the point in the film, y'know? Like they overdid it.

Facilitator: That's what bothers me, too, I think. A bit too pat there. I have problems with a couple of other places like it. Is that what you meant when you said you got bored?

George: Yeah. I had to wait for the whole flower-smelling bit to end. I knew what was going to happen. It was like a sticky love scene in a good action flick.

John: I didn't even see that flower until he got to it. I think it's perfectly natural, especially in his situation. He'd been through a lot. Besides, it sets up the next action sequence, where he's running again. I think maybe all straight action would get boring.

Facilitator: You weren't bored, and you didn't think it was corny?

John: Maybe if I saw it again it might be. But not then. I mean, you've seen it a hundred times, so you don't like it, right?

Facilitator: I'm not exactly sure why. It seems set up to me, too, but you're right—maybe it's because I've seen it so much. Yet the ending still impresses me.

SILENCE

Facilitator: George, one more thing. I can see how you thought it was overdone and a little contrived, which was how you saw it. But why did you say faggy? Apparently you didn't really feel he was faggy, from what you said a couple of minutes ago.

George: Well, not really. It's just that a guy sniffing a flower like that is usually considered—well. . . .

Facilitator: By most people?

George: Yeah. Not in his case, but usually.

Facilitator: How about in this class?

George: Yeah. Definitely.

At this point the facilitator might check out the rest of the class' feelings about the subject. Girls might express feelings that are very different from boys', and the whole subject of hippies and flower-children might arise. The facilitator would probably want to return to the question of why George used the word "faggy," and particularly whether he felt obligated to use it because of his perception of social norms, however legitimate the action might have been in the film. Once the issue becomes clear, the facilitator can help the class examine available options, offering his own feelings about the subject. Possibly George's perception of the social norms is exaggerated, but others may feel similarly. If the facilitator wishes, he can also examine other instances of how norms operate in the class, but he would probably be teaching rather than facilitating if he did. It is far more effective to deal with such issues when they are actually occurring rather than abstractly.

These matters can be related to the film itself. A digression from the topic of discussion supports growing awareness of the class' responses to the film, and even of the theme of the film—a general objective of the academic teacher—efficiently. Instead of or in addition to Bob's abstract summary of the theme in the first example, comments would probably be more likely to relate to the students' actual feelings and concerns.

FACILITATING, MODERATING, OR TEACHING

In order to facilitate, a teacher must do more than moderate discussion. A moderator typically maintains and encourages orderly, sometimes lively discussion, trying to get everyone involved while sticking to the topic. Usually he does not actively participate in this discussion. Instead, he clarifies by asking probing questions; he summarizes; he indicates new directions for discussion; and he focuses attention upon particular points raised. A facilitator, on the other hand, is much more personally involved in the discussion. Carl Rogers specifies three characteristics of the effective facilitator of learning: genuineness or realness; caring and empathy; and a quality of prizing, accepting, and trusting students. In addition, he constantly tries to communicate what is going on in himself at the moment, even if it does not fit the stereotype of what a teacher should think and feel.

The extent to which a teacher wants to try to behave more like a facilitator than a moderator depends upon his ultimate aim. Clearly there are advantages to moderating a discussion. The discussion is likely to progress in an orderly fashion and many students will be able to contribute profitably. A moderated discussion need not be a dull one, either. Such a class does not, though, have the climate of freedom, trust, and openness that a facilitator's class can develop. The kind of learning that takes place in a moderator's class, therefore, is less likely to be *personally* significant, for it usually reflects the typical concerns and objectives of a regular curriculum, or at least the teacher's concerns. Students working with a moderator will probably raise and deal with the kinds of issues and questions they are usually expected to treat. The moderator forecloses options, particularly the option of student-based and derived, experiential learning.

Facilitation, on the other hand, encourages collaboration. Both the facilitator and the students may experiment, within generally agreed-upon ground rules, with different ways of interacting. The ground rules themselves should be flexible, so if students find that discussions bog down without more directive leadership, they can negotiate to change the procedures. However, they may discover that they need much less structure than they are used to. When they are examining complex issues or need a common vocabulary to discuss a film more efficiently, they can call on the facilitator or someone else (perhaps another student) to provide the information, perhaps in a very tightly structured way.

This structured presentation is teaching: what we are most used to, and what we must use more judiciously when we have films in the classroom. In this view, teaching means providing information and asking questions in such a way that students come up with particular answers. It is frequently the most efficient way to cover a discrete body of material, but because it can frustrate movement toward more desirable ends or even become an end in itself, it should be considered a last resort. Students routinely receive so much teaching that other kinds of relationships with adults in a school may well be worth the sacrificed efficiency.

To follow consistently the principle of collaborative design of film classes, you should ask for feedback from students and others in order to be sure that teaching, if you are using it, is actually accomplishing the desired objective. Often, after teaching has continued for a while, the group may need to clarify its definition of the problem. It may see another, more pertinent objective for which teaching may be inappropriate.

It is difficult to facilitate, to avoid teaching, because we habitually reward comments that "advance" discussion toward preordained conclusions or in preordained directions. To listen fully, to be sensitive to nonverbal cues, and to be open to a wide range of unexpected ways of seeing are the most challenging tasks that a teacher—or anyone, for that matter—can assume. To do so, I believe, is to commit oneself to personal growth in his professional life.

There are no hard and fast rules separating teaching, moderating, and facilitating, beyond the general guidelines I have already mentioned. I can only suggest that you experiment with facilitation as frequently and deliberately as you can until you believe you have tried it enough to be able to choose fairly. At least you can extend your repertoire of teaching behaviors. It may be necessary to modify an approach at times, though, especially when you feel that you're floundering.

When a discussion flags, a teacher often searches for cues that might touch off provocative discussion topics. He may maintain a rich stockpile of topics or leads to heat a tepid conversation. Even though the leads may not necessarily address students' present concerns, they may evoke common, enduring ones and get the teacher off the hook. This kind of strategy, however, is not facilitative. The priority is not upon the present feelings and ideas in the class, but upon what the teacher would like them to be. Rather than accepting the students, the teacher is trying to make them feel and think differently; that is, to have a hot discussion. A behavioral view of teaching, of course, states that the purpose of teaching is to make students behave differently by rewarding them accordingly; the provocative questions, then, are designed to stimulate kids to behave in ways that the teacher can reward. A behavioral view may be appropriate to some teaching situations, but not here. The question here is one of ends; a hot discussion should not be an end in itself.

Learning to facilitate not only takes time and willingness to change; systematic effort to change is needed as well. Feedback from students and friends on my own progress and problems in learning to facilitate, for example, indicates that I still have trouble genuinely accepting how students feel. I am perceived as occasionally trying to get them to see the way I see and to become excited in the way that I or other students have been. Recently I have been experimenting with my own behavior, trying not to impose my own notions of vitality on the discussion, paying closer attention to what students have actually said, checking to see how they actually feel instead of raising volatile subjects in order to provoke the feelings or ideas I want. I find the most difficulty when I have spectators in the room, especially a student's guest who has come expecting an unusually good class, or a friend who has heard me say it's a great class. I also feel the temptation when I notice that a student is uninvolved. It includes a few risks but I've consistently found that if I can discover where that student or class is—by asking directly—we can work together toward a more involving class.

To illustrate, suppose the class discussing *An Occurrence at Owl Creek Bridge* has a few students who seem to be out of it temporarily. The key to facilitating involvement with such students is to be nonthreatening, nonevaluative. Do not convey, as many teachers do, a sense that you disapprove or are punishing the student by exposing him.

Facilitator:	Jim, what are you . . .
Jim:	Huh?
Facilitator:	I've been wondering what you're feeling over there.
Jim:	I don't know.
Facilitator:	You were with us before and now you seem to be somewhere else. You turned off somewhere.
Jim:	Okay, I'm sorry.
Facilitator:	There's nothing wrong with that, but I'd like to know when you left.
Jim:	When you got off into something about the thing with a flower—I don't know.
Facilitator:	We were into that for quite a while. You got bored?
Jim:	Yeah, a little.
Facilitator:	Okay, we're off that now and at loose ends. Would you like to get us going again with something, or do you feel at a dead end, too?

Jim: I don't know. There's a lot more in the movie. We
               got off on that flower.

George: John's a flower freak.

Jim: Let's get back to the images like when we started.
               I'm sick of flowers.

Facilitator: Okay, no more flowers. Give us an image.

Jim: Trees.

Joanne: Branch in the water.

Oscar: Hanging from the bridge.

Jim: Far away. Camera's moving. Sound of birds.

John: At the beginning, too, those birds.

Alice: Only a second went by, really.

George: Weird.

Bob: Birds, trees, bugs, flowers — all images of life, right?

Facilitator: Rushing current.

Jim: Still water.

The image-sound skim, then, is a comfortable setting for involving students again because it is so apparently simple and yet provides all the information you need to communicate genuinely and personally with students while still addressing the material at hand, the movie.

The image-sound skim accommodates all three of the major approaches to film study mentioned at the start of this chapter, as well as approaches based on the objectives of subject-matter disciplines.

It helps students study the film as art because it concentrates on the concrete aesthetic details of style, composition, and content. A thorough study of outstanding films depends upon the students' exploring the individual aesthetic of each of those films. Furthermore, observing the evolution of specific ways of solving different kinds of artistic problems illuminates any study of film history.

THE USE OF TECHNIQUES

Nothing dulls our attention more than clichés. All approaches to film study treat this problem. Since the exercise sensitizes students to all kinds and contexts of cinematic expression, it prepares them to begin distinguishing originality from triteness. As they

discover that one technique suggests countless other examples
(e.g., bombarding the audience with a rapid barrage of images)
they become less impressed by a fancy technique and begin to
question intuitively as well as intellectually why it'is being used.

It takes surprisingly little time for students to develop this
sensitivity. Instead of saying, "Great technique!" they begin asking,
"How's he using it?" For instance, Arthur Lipsett's short film
Very Nice, Very Nice is a frantic montage of photography accompanied by a fragmented soundtrack — snatches of conversation,
sounds, and music, all associated with daily absurdities and tensions of contemporary life, and The Bomb. The form of the film
itself reflects its implicit "content." Whether a viewer considers the
film blatantly didactic, satirical, merely clever, or bewildering and
irritating depends largely on how familiar he is with the technique.

In the past few years, Lipsett's technique has become a stock
device in television; e.g., in short spots for upcoming network programs, in "hooks" for adventure shows, in countless ads for soft
drinks and toys, and in campaign spots. The technique rivets our
attention just long enough for the ad to make its pitch; even if we
are irritated, we rarely turn away. In any case, whether we are
irritated or attracted, the name of the product will be indelibly
pounded into our memories.

Whether this technique works in *The Loneliness of the Long
Distance Runner, The Pawnbroker, Easy Rider, Allures, An
American Time Capsule, Fail Safe,* or countless student films
raises a host of other questions. For instance, does a student using
this technqiue treat his material sensitively, or is he merely con-
structing a flashy Celluloid scrapbook? Students cannot communicate with film language unless they not only are immersed in it
but are also sensitive to its specific limitations and possibilities.
While we want students to express themselves originally, we cannot expect them to avoid clichés unless they can sense them
intuitively.

The image-sound skim helps them develop this capacity, so
that when they see zany films like *Morgan!* they can begin to identify pretension or pointlessness as they experience it. Many current movies utilize unusual techniques for no apparent reason other
than to appear modern. Once students can begin to compare the
sequences independently and automatically to other examples
they have assimilated in skimming exercises, they will begin to
join that discriminating "great audience" we all hope for — an
audience that has developed the capacity not to be fooled intellectually or emotionally.

COMMERCIALS

Commercials are particularly useful in developing this sort of sophistication. The American Television Commercials Festival rents for about $35.00 a 40-minute reel of the award-winning television commercials of any given year. You may show the film as many times as you wish for a period of two weeks. There is, I believe, no richer resource for film language than these films, because they are so concise and so expertly executed. As students watch these familiar shorts, recall images and sounds, and express feelings and random associations, they begin seeing instead of merely watching.

Students will watch these films repeatedly; there are few films with such universal appeal. As they become immersed in this intense and concise film language, they begin to identify precisely how specific techniques are used. When they watch other films, in or out of school, they will associate shots, scenes, and sequences with these examples. Then, once the associations become explicit, they can begin to formulate critical distinctions.

The use of commercials is particularly appropriate to investigating McLuhan's controversial notions of "hot" and "cool" media. A hot medium, he contends, has high definition, is intense, and requires less from us than a cool medium, which demands our participation. Thus, print is hot, speech is cool; similarly, movies are hotter than television because the imperfect, smaller image of television demands more of our attention.

As Kenneth Boulding points out, McLuhan's ideas, though tremendously significant, may be imprecise in some respects. One problem, Boulding says, is that McLuhan attributes the significance of a medium solely to its physical form without considering the importance of its social context.[3]

Social context is integral to the study of commercials. Showing commercials without image-sound skimming and examining and sharing feelings and associations usually does not markedly increase students' sensitivity to film language. Without the exercise, they watch rather than see. Of course, the commercials can be examined systematically, like a grammar text, to teach film language, but that approach soon becomes drudgery for many students.

[3]*In* Stearn, G. E. (Ed.): *McLuhan: Hot and Cool.* New York: The Dial Press, 1967, pp. 56–64.

PERIOD FILMS

Still another related approach is to study the films of a given period—say, the Thirties or Forties—as a means of discovering how the social forces of that time influenced and were reflected in popular film art. Mark Phillips has described, for instance, how *King Kong* and Disney's *The Three Little Pigs* illuminate a study of the Depression (see Appendix II). Further, in *Films and Feeling* Raymond Durgnat has shown that escapist movies reflect the social realities and tensions that they are trying to escape. In this approach the skimming exercise can be useful in comparing the students' reactions to those of the audiences which first saw the film. One group that I observed, for instance, insisted that *King Kong* could be used today as a metaphor for Black Power, a suggestion that Bosley Crowther[4] makes in his book *The Great Films*. The comment emerged, however, from random associations in an image-sound skim rather than from a determined search for possible symbols.

The process they used to reach their conclusion, in fact, was the same as that of a good critic like Crowther, who is able to recognize, accept, and develop the implications of his feelings about an experience.

THE LITERARY APPROACH

I have seen the image-sound skim make the crucial difference between academic discussion and lively communication in many social studies and English classes, using Tony Richardson's *The Loneliness of the Long Distance Runner*. While observing and conducting classes with literally all kinds of students, I have been struck by how frequently students have been asked to respond to the movie in the same ways. Most classes are asked to examine the interplay among plot, theme, setting, and characterization, citing specific incidents or scenes as evidence—a procedure that usually works well in literature classes. This literary approach seems appropriate at first glance, because there is a definite story line in the film; in fact, the film is adapted from a short novel. However, teachers assume that the students have a common sphere of experience; this is just not so. The barrier of print may be down, but plenty of perceptual fences remain. As a result, the conversation

---

[4]Bosley Crowther was film critic for *The New York Times* for many years.

tends to become increasingly abstract, removed from the experience of the film itself. Not surprisingly, discussions of this and other allegedly sure-fire movies are often less than electric.

More important, such sessions generate many incidental learnings that combine to kill the film experience. For example, students learn that ideas, not feelings, count in class; that there are only a few "right" interpretations of a movie; that the teacher knows what really matters in a movie; that if you get too involved in a movie, you won't be able to answer important questions; that you'd better be on the ball during a movie because there's no way to grind out a better grade by studying harder, no way to review; and finally, if you want to understand a movie, read the book.

ADVANTAGES OF THE IMAGE-SOUND SKIM

By contrast, a teacher using the image-sound skim discovers that students not only perceive the film differently, but are often confused by flashbacks, miss much dialogue because of the difficult dialect, are occasionally bored, and may feel generally confused about the film. Despite these problems, though, they often agree that the film is nevertheless a moving experience. The potential value in their discussion, then, is in finding out the different ways they found it moving. By using the skim, we can touch directly upon a central aesthetic feature of movies — that a movie can communicate without having been understood.

Students can often find structure or sense in a film after an image-sound skim. In addition, they can clarify questions, some of which may reveal inconsistencies in the film and raise major critical issues. For instance, Pauline Kael maintains that in *The Loneliness of the Long Distance Runner* Richardson confuses his audience when he editorially has Colin, the protagonist, expound a series of half-baked socialistic statements, implying a whole set of philosophical motives that muddle our view of the rest of the film, including the climax. During one skimming exercise it became evident that students were confused, too. Several either forgot the scene or could not relate it to the rest of the film. As one boy put it, the scene seemed like a bad commercial. This reaction led to a discussion of preachy-ness in the film. Identifying which images and sequences struck students as contrived and which did not — for whatever reasons — enabled the group to examine specifically the differences between the ways the director conveyed his own ideas, and the ways in which he shaped his material to convey a personal vision. This is a highly sophisticated distinction that would probably be beyond the students' critical capacities if they were not speaking in terms of the concrete details of the film which comprised both content and style.

The skimming procedure recalls the crucial yet elusive sense of the present in a film experience, but recalling images, sequences, and sounds is not the same as re-experiencing them directly. Although a teacher may be able to rescreen a segment of a feature film or may be able to repeat a short in its entirety, most of the time students must rely on memory to provide raw material for discussion. Inevitably their recollections are selective and at times distort the original material. As long as everyone realizes that this distortion is taking place everyone sees the same movie differently, the distortions actually become an advantage; they provide information the students can use to compare ways of seeing, including the filmmaker's way of seeing.

This use of the class' collective memory is substantially different from the use of memory in an academic setting, in which memorization supposedly insures that the students "know" the material cold. Whether they responded sensitively or perceptively to the material or whether they found it personally significant is not generally considered to be knowledge. However, these matters are knowledge. As Harold Taylor has stressed in *Art and the Intellect*, the effect that art has upon us is experiential knowledge, which is certainly as important for mental growth as factual material is.

EXPERIENCE: THE COMPLETE PICTURE

Whatever we say we believe, we typically behave in schools as if we consider knowledge to be a clearly defined set of ideas and facts, demonstrable only in numbers and words. Educators do not usually sanction nonverbal experience, especially in the arts, as forms of knowledge, and a large part of the legitimacy that film has acquired is due to its relationship to verbal forms of knowledge: the novel and drama. However, the full experience of the film itself, especially the nonverbal elements, is the source of its major value in learning. To minimize the value of this nonverbal experience by neglecting it in the activity of the classroom is to teach students to devalue all but a narrow range of experiences.

The underground, or counter-culture, has taught students to value these forms of knowledge, often in ways which promote equally distorted attitudes and values. Film educators have an opportunity and a responsibility, then, to foster the integration of these attitudes and values by supporting the value of a full range of experiential knowledge, verbal and nonverbal, that is available in movies.

   This exercise can fail as surely as a boring lecture if the teacher is unreal or dishonest, or if he is playing his own game. One of the most typical ways of perverting the exercise is to reward certain comments which fit what the teacher is really driving at. For example:

Teacher:	What else did you notice?
George:	Branch floating in the water when he looked down.
Teacher:	Was it a real branch, or was he just imagining it?
George:	It was real. I'm pretty sure.
Teacher:	How did you know?
George:	Well, it was before he fell, and he was looking down.
Teacher:	Uh-huh. Joanne?
Joanne:	When he was running down the road and fell.
Teacher:	Was that fantasy?
Joanne:	Sure. That whole chase was just in his mind.
Teacher:	Did you know at the time?
Joanne:	Oh, no. I mean, I thought maybe they were right behind him or were heading him off the other way.
Teacher:	Mm-hm. Any other images? Alice?
Alice:	That huge gate right after he fell.
Teacher:	And what about that gate did you notice?
Alice:	Sort of strange. It opened all by itself.
Teacher:	Good! Did that seem unreal to you?
Alice:	Yes. Like the Pearly Gates or something.
Teacher:	Good. Do you think that's one of the signals that this is really a fantasy?
Alice:	Yeah. I wondered at the time.
Oscar:	I thought it was phony. He almost blew the whole film with that shot.
Teacher:	What made it phony?
Oscar:	It gave away what was happening. That whole business with the gate should have been cut.
Teacher:	Were there any other devices that showed you fantasy? How about near the very end, when he is running toward the camera, over and over?

Oscar:	But they didn't give it away like the bit with the gates.
Teacher:	Why not, if the scene was not entirely realistic? It was dream-like, wasn't it?
Oscar:	I don't know. It just didn't.
Teacher:	Oscar has raised a good point, though. Is Enrico consistent in this movie? And how important is consistency in this movie?

SILENCE

Despite good intentions to guide the class toward examining specific devices in the film, to give coherence to the image-skim, and to urge Oscar to explain his judgment logically, the teacher may have killed the film. Not only did he turn the exercise into a guessing game run by his rules, and ignore Oscar's strong feeling, but he annihilated Oscar in debate. All of his early questions lead to a single point, one which is important to a full understanding of the film, but one which the students, particularly Oscar, are not *primarily* interested in. When he subversively insists that they direct their attention to his point, the students are learning that what they care about doesn't count. Oscar's strong criticism may in fact be justified. By debating fine points, the teacher merely proves that he can get the upper hand in an argument. Instead of using questions to probe, he uses them to stab. His implicit objectives might look great on a lesson plan, but they are meaningless, even destructive, if not reached humanistically.

There are many ways to tap the knowledge that a student or class has acquired. One way teachers typically try to create a common sphere of experience is with a study guide, a set of questions to provide a mind-set about the movie, and occasionally several suggestions of particular things to look for. The study guide, though, is inappropriate to the aims I have been describing. To condition students about a film beforehand is to prejudice them and to eliminate chances to investigate not only what the filmmaker has conveyed but also how the students have individually and collectively perceived it. To ask students to see a movie in a particular light prevents them from seeing it in its own light.

The following chapter describes a body of procedures growing from the image-sound skim approach. Although these procedures might be used for a variety of purposes, the fundamental emphasis is to help students become more fully aware of the particular and common ways in which they perceive and respond to a film and, by extension, to their other personal experiences.

4

BAG IS GAB SPELLED BACKWARDS: A DOZEN DEVICES

What follows will merely be a bag of tricks unless used to help the student concentrate upon seeing, upon feeling, and upon remaining in touch with his experience of the movie in order to develop his own meaning from it.

Three major guidelines govern these procedures: (1) Assume little or nothing about how students will experience a film, (2) treat style as content, and (3) ask for and offer feelings about the film.

MAKE NO ASSUMPTIONS

Most assumptions, whether apparently justified or not, are dangerous in film study, for no matter how long or earnestly you have taught, you cannot anticipate how students will experience a movie. Despite all the talk of how kids love movies, for example, countless teachers have discovered that no film is sure-fire. Two famous movies starring Marlon Brando, *The Wild One* and *On the Waterfront,* frequently shown because they have such obvious relationships to each other and to kids' interests, carry no guarantees. Ben Snyder of the Cranbrook Upward Bound program reported disappointment in both films; apparently, to the kids in his program, Brando has lost his "cool," and the dialogue now seems stilted. He also says that the boys in the program found it difficult to relate to another of the sure-fire films, *The Loneliness of the Long Distance Runner.*[1]

I, too, have seen these films fail in the classroom, but I have also seen them succeed. The key is not, I believe, primarily in the selection of the film. To run a film program on the basis of assump-

---

[1]Snyder, Ben: Upward-Bound and A-Better Chance Programs and the movies. *The Independent School Bulletin.* Vol. 27, No. 3, February, 1968, p. 74.

Figure 13. *Judoka.*
Courtesy Pathe-Contemporary Films/McGraw-Hill

tions that some films work and others don't is a mistake. For instance, in an inner city class of nonacademic eighth grade students, another teacher and I used *The Wild One* for entertainment after we had been disappointed with the poor response to a supposedly sure-fire western, *3:10 to Yuma,* and suddenly found ourselves in a lively, sophisticated bull session lasting nearly three hours. The students began comparing and contrasting the two films by relating them pointedly to issues of values, responsibility, and order in their own school, class, and personal lives. The success of the class depended not on the film itself or on the issues involved, but on the resonances between the films and their immediate concerns.

Whether using a short personal documentary like *Judoka* or a sensuous, poetic film like *Dream of the Wild Horses,* I can never even approximately predict audience response. I have to wait instead for directions to emerge from the students as we explore concerns or associations which the films evoke. Age, past experience with film, and expertise does not seem to matter, either. Showing *Dream of the Wild Horses* to educational film producers, I met strong criticism because the film "has a terrible soundtrack, shows cruelty to animals, and is pointless"; several college students, on the other hand, seized upon the notion that the film simulated a drug trip. Although both discussions were eventually productive, they took vastly different directions because the spectators had such different frames of reference.

There is, then, a perceptual view of "relevance." Film study suggests that what is most relevant to students is not a particular or universal social, psychological, religious, or philosophical theme, or even any apparently practical lesson, but rather the process of making the students aware of their separate and common ways of perceiving and responding. This process is basic to all concerns and values, and an intense film experience provides one kind of opportunity to examine them systematically in the classroom. The examination itself, though, cannot be reduced to a codified set of classroom procedures, for its success depends upon facilitation — the teacher's ability to communicate his desire to relate to his students as openly, honestly, and personally as possible, exploring the common fund of experience of the film.

CONTENT IS STYLE

The second guideline, the aesthetic theory that content is style, is closely related to the first, and helps us to relate our personal viewpoints to the content of the film. It means that the pictorial values in a film — the details, the elements of rhythm, color, pace, and composition — *are* the content, even though this content may be difficult to describe in words. As Durgnat points out, the actor's facial expressions and gestures, the director's spatial relationships, and the way a cameraman may have caught a particular shade of gray all combine to communicate an experience forcefully.[2] Although these details are often called "style" and theme or emotion is called "content," the two concepts are actually inseparable. In addition, the spectator deduces the con-

---

[2]Durgnat, R.: *Films and Feelings.* Cambridge: The M.I.T. Press, 1967, Chapter 2.

tent from what he sees; the emotion is in *him*, not on the screen. This is why so many people often disagree about the content of a film, and why among critics there are such wide differences of opinion on every aspect of the movies. Opinions depend upon the spectator's personal prism. Since every film experience is different, it is virtually impossible to predict the content of a film beforehand. Only by getting inside the film experience itself, getting to the details of style and relating them to our own feelings and responses, can we discover the content.

FEELINGS

The third guideline, to ask for and offer feelings, is the best way I know to begin facilitating, for immediately the discussion becomes personal, not academic. It is often difficult for us to state how we feel, because we are so accustomed to saying what we think ("I feel that...."), yet thoughts alone—particularly in the beginning—will quickly leave the experience far behind. Offering your own feelings entails more than setting an example for students to follow; it means consistently participating in the discussion, not simply guiding it.

The following procedures, like the image-sound skim, are designed to help students discover the content of a film by discovering the content in themselves.

EXAMINE FEELINGS SURROUNDING WHATEVER INTERESTS STUDENTS AT THE MOMENT

This procedure is derived from a theory of Gestalt psychology that states whatever concerns us most will dominate our thoughts and feelings. That is, although the director of a film tries to communicate significance by many cinematic means, we assign different degrees of importance to various elements depending upon our past experiences, factors in our immediate environment, and our views of ourselves.

A short film widely used to demonstrate this principle is *Eye of the Beholder*, which clearly, if simplistically, illustrates how different people may see the same individual very differently, depending upon their frames of reference. In this film, an artist is seen variously as a good boy, a ladies' man, a gangster, a lunatic, a murderer, and a square. Shown prior to a series of other films, it

Figure 14. *The Loneliness of the Long Distance Runner.*

Photo courtesy Walter Read 16

may be used to acquaint a class with the principle behind the discussion procedure.

Several examples illustrate variations on this procedure. The first shows how it helped stimulate a discussion of *The Loneliness of the Long Distance Runner* (see Fig. 14). During a flashback in the film, Colin is wandering around the house and picks up a package of cigarettes. Seeing that only one cigarette remains, he returns the pack without taking the cigarette. It is a simple, easily unnoticed detail which nevertheless suggests a great deal about Colin's personal values and acquires additional significance when considered in the context of his crime—burglary—and his later struggle with values in reform school. Although many spectators, including me, missed that detail, a student who had felt a need to smoke during the movie spotted it immediately, and told us why.

During the short scene he was acutely aware of what he would probably have done in Colin's place, and his feelings about that emerged during an image-sound skim. Eventually the group focused on Colin's personal values and examined their own values as well. In this way, the single student's personal, seemingly irrelevant desire for a cigarette provided a way to study both the movie and the students' personal values.

Even though this way of treating feelings about any random image or sound seems at first glance to sidetrack the class, it is one of the fastest ways to study how the film communicates. Because any detail or incident in a movie usually reflects or reinforces other details, scenes, and sequences, you should be able to start anywhere and relate the part to the whole. Even if the detail is

Figure 15. Corral.
Courtesy Pathe-Contemporary Films/McGraw-Hill

inconsistent, that very fact highlights the surrounding structure of the film.

Examining feelings about the film *Corral* shown to a group of allegedly uneducable, unruly boys in a foster home led to one of the most rewarding discussions of personal concerns I have experienced in film study. A social worker had invited me to visit with some movies in order to see if film could reach a group of boys aged 11 to 17 who had resisted all other forms of classroom activity.

Corral is a short, impressionistic, nondialogue documentary describing how a cowboy saddles a half-broken horse. It is often used in film study classes to illustrate superbly concise editing, particularly in the way the camera isolates the horse to be saddled, maintains tension, and conveys the gentleness and strength of the cowboy. Of course, I did not begin with a dry discussion of editing but instead explored moments of interest, starting with the simple questions "What did you see?" and "How did you feel?"

The boys began talking randomly about how the cowboy *made* the horse obey. Probing their remarks, I tried to focus attention on what specific shots showed how he "made" the horse obey—in other words, what they saw and how they felt about it, rather than generalities. One boy insisted that the horse was afraid of the cowboy.

"He wasn't afraid. He was just going to keep him off his back," another replied.

"He was scared of him, all right."

"No—he was twice as big as that guy. That horse wasn't scared of *nobody*."

"He was scared."

"What did you see that showed you he was scared?" I asked.

"When they showed his gun. The horse knew he'd better shape up or get shot in the head."

However, there is no gun in the film; the boy simply imagined it. A quick survey showed that more than one boy thought there was a gun, though some were certain there was none; others were uncertain.

We eventually solved the problem by showing part of the film again, and it was simple and logical enough to explain the mistake by saying that we are so used to seeing cowboys wear guns in movies that we naturally assumed it in this one. However, the question remained: If there was no gun, why did the horse eventually behave?

Answer: "The horse was scared the guy would bust his leg with the rope."

"He wasn't gonna bust his leg—you can't ride a horse with a busted leg. Then you'll have to shoot him."

"He was scared he'd whip him with it."

"What did you see that showed that?" I asked.

It became evident, after over an hour's discussion (uneducable, unruly kids?), that the boys simply found it confusing to watch the kind of discipline they had witnessed because it was not part of their usual experience. They were not "wrong" about the movie; they were simply describing their perceptions. When we examined the concrete experience itself, the actual images which showed the cowboy's controlled, firm gentleness and the horse's growing trust, they began to see the film—and themselves—differently.

Their changed view of themselves emerged during discussion

Figure 16. *Tamer of Wild Horses.*
Courtesy Pathe-Contemporary Films/McGraw-Hill

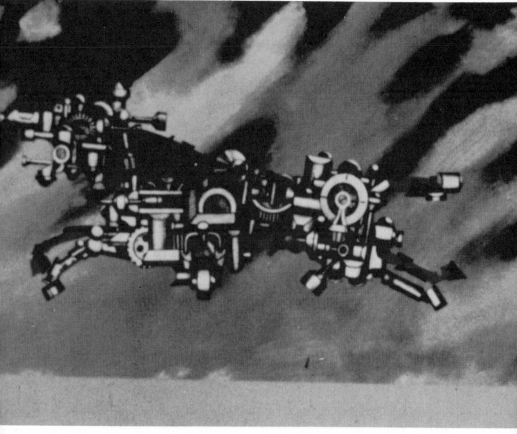

Figure 17. *Tamer of Wild Horses.*

Courtesy Pathe-Contemporary Films/McGraw-Hill

of their feelings about me and how I had controlled them. I asked them to discuss their feelings about the film and about their participation in the discussion and their relationsip to me.

One boy said, "You're lucky you ain't a teacher."

"Why is that?"

"We don't talk to no teachers."

"Well, in fact I am a teacher."

Suddenly, the mood changed, as if the boys had been hoodwinked. We resolved the subsequent encounter by going directly back to the behavior of the group and to the film itself: What had they said about the cowboy's gun? Do all cowboys have guns? Do all teachers act the same? How have I acted? Exactly what have I done? What have you done and felt in the last two hours?

Since then I have used the movie along with *Dream of the Wild Horses* to train teachers, for teachers often have feelings simi-

Figure 18. Tamer of Wild Horses.
Courtesy Pathe-Contemporary Films/McGraw-Hill

lar to those of the boys, but from a different standpoint (see Figs. 1 and 2). After seeing *Dream of the Wild Horses* I ask teachers to write freely about the film. Their writing invariably reveals a great deal about their own views of teaching, of students, and of learning. For instance, one teacher may see the horses as wild, uncontrollable, and dangerous, while another may see them as free, beautiful, nonthreatening. They compare their feelings about *Corral* to feelings about *Dream of the Wild Horses,* and then examine specific instances of discipline problems they have experienced, case studies, and role playing.

A recent short film *Tamer of Wild Horses* adds still another excellent resource that uses horses (see Figs. 16, 17, 18). This Yugoslavian animated short film invites several interpretations, but its application to teaching is especially intriguing. The film begins with a little man who ropes stallions, rides them until they break, and sends them off to graze with the rest of his growing herd. One day he discovers a monstrous horse, so large that his hoof alone dwarfs the man. He tries to ride the horse anyway, but when he swats him, the horse becomes charged with electricity, grows red hot, and sprouts a huge array of complicated technological devices to get rid of his rider. The man is determined, however, and stays on. Finally, the horse sprouts a gigantic pair of wings, the mood of the film changes, and the horse—Pegasus now—glides into the clouds with the man on his back.

On one level the film is a metaphor for the growth from autocratic teaching to humanistic education. At first the teacher ropes and defeats his students; he tames them into submissive, spiritless creatures. If he uses media and technology in his classroom, he may find his role and status threatened. Finally, though, if he hangs in there with his students, humanistically, they may carry him to Olympus.

Examining feelings about *Leaf*, a film frequently shown in English classes to stimulate writing and to explore possible symbolism, shows how film may actually do the class a disservice if students do not explore their feelings honestly.

Leaf portrays the journey of a single leaf, the last on the tree, in Yosemite as the wind pulls it from the branch, takes it over steep cliffs, and tumbles it through the air. It falls into a mountain stream, and finally, soaked, flattened, almost abstract, it floats slowly into darkness.

The film may evoke a variety of emotions, but some of the comments may be mildly dishonest, statements of feeling that the film invites but does not actually evoke. When a student says that he felt lonely at a certain point or that the film is "about" loneliness or solitude, when he did not in fact feel that emotion, he may be saying that the single leaf is a cue (a possible symbol of loneliness) or he may be playing the old classroom game. In fact, the leaf is merely an image on the screen, and there should not be a premium on saying that the director succeeded in evoking a particular response if he did not. Nor is it necessarily praiseworthy to say that the leaf is a symbol of loneliness or happiness or the life cycle if it actually strikes the viewer as a trite number about "a day in the life (or death) of a leaf." By probing these statements about a film and by supporting statements of feelings of all kinds, however iconoclastic, we can help students distinguish between what they think they ought to say, or what the filmmaker apparently intended to show, and what they actually felt and thought.

Surely this determined honesty is prerequisite to sound academic criticism, no matter what additional theoretical tools may be required, but more importantly, this honesty is central to personally significant learning.

Students need to become aware of these mild forms of self-deception; they need to feel that they owe a film — or a book — nothing; and they need to become aware that whatever they felt or thought is not only legitimate but also valuable and worth sharing. The difficulty comes in stating what one actually felt or thought rather than what he thinks he *ought* to have felt. When we are constantly worried about what we ought to feel, we deny our feelings and train ourselves to be unable to accept either our own feelings or those of others. It is one more way of learning not to accept ourselves as we are, or others as they are.

I am not overstating the case, for schooling (as opposed to education) constantly encourages dishonesty about feelings. Because the process of learning to disguise our feelings is subtle, ongoing, and destructive, we should take special pains to counteract that process in the classroom. Classes are not designed to admit more than a narrow range of feelings, and that range is generally prescribed. In many cases feelings may seem dangerous or may threaten the orderly progress of discussion.

When is it appropriate and desirable to deal with here-and-now feelings in a film class? This is a generally controversial issue presently being examined systematically in schools and universities developing curricula for affective education. You must, of course, judge what level of feeling is appropriate to examine, and you must never force students to reveal feelings if you are not sure you want to deal with those feelings completely. Here-and-now feelings are usually appropriate when they involve low risk and facilitate communication. The feelings are nevertheless there; the issue before you is how to deal with them.

An example occurred in one training session which I conducted in an inner city junior high school for paraprofessionals training to become licensed teachers. The session was proceeding mildly well, but with moderate energy at best, as students discussed *Boundary Lines*, a didactic film about barriers which all people construct — particularly the boundaries drawn by prejudice. The film shows how a line can either separate men or, by becoming a circle, join them.

Someone pointed out that the group was sitting in a circle and seemed to reflect the values in the film. Using this remark as a cue, I said that I felt a certain barrier between myself and the class, that the discussion seemed unusually polite and intellectual, and that I was being exceptionally teacher-like and felt uneasy in an unfamiliar setting. I said that I wondered whether they too sensed boundary lines inside our circle.

At that point the class came alive. Many feelings emerged, and we were able to deal with them and change the climate and direction of the discussion. Because I phrased the question in relation to myself and the class, and because I invited feedback and its consequences, the remarks were appropriate. Many barriers were obvious. For instance, I was the only white person in the room. One student who had not talked until then told me how I had upset her from the beginning by what she considered unprofessional behavior. Others expressed their feelings about my credentials, my clothes, my speech, and the process of discussion — the orderly raising of hands, the strained feelings when others interrupted, and so forth. One talkative man launched into an impassioned speech about how no barriers whatsoever existed, but it was neither necessary nor appropriate to challenge him. We were communicating on a more involving level than before, and at the same time dealing with the substance of the film.

THE HERE-AND-NOW WHEEL

The here-and-now wheel is a device you can use in a brief time to accomplish several purposes. It can be used to inform you and your students of the specific variations in class climate, it can be used to examine strong, unexpressed feelings, and it can be used to identify feelings about particular parts of a film.

To construct a here-and-now wheel, a student draws several spokes in a wheel and writes a feeling he has at that moment on each spoke, filling as many spokes as he chooses. Then the feelings can be shared and discussed. Thus, one wheel might read: bored, impatient, irritated, tense, confused; another might read: relaxed, interested, energetic.

You can use the here-and-now wheel in a discussion when you want a reading on how things are going, especially if you have an uncomfortable feeling that you can't put your finger on. Once feelings are out, you can deal directly with them and begin building a productive discussion. The advantage of having students write the comments is that they then have the option to reveal or withhold what they wish; eventually students may be able to state feelings without being asked. In short, the here-and-now wheel is a device to help you and your students collaborate in making the classroom experience all they would like it to become.

The wheel is often useful in midscreening. At given points students jot down a feeling or set of feelings on a wheel and keep them for discussion, or you can freeze a frame and have the students jot down a wheel. Later the wheels can be compared.

The device is especially useful with a film that attempts to evoke a succession of feelings, such as *Leaf*, or a feature film in which a great deal of time elapses between important sequences. If a student watching *Leaf* feels joy or lightness at one point, he may be surprised to discover that another student was irritated at that moment. In this way you can deal directly with a large number of feelings about a given moment in a film, all of which shed light on the important ideational and aesthetic issues which those feelings implicitly raise.

TREAT FEELINGS AS CONTENT

A corollary of the above techniques, this procedure can be useful with all films, but especially with documentaries. If students can study documentaries in terms of feelings, their ideas about all movies will become much more firmly rooted in their emotional as well as their intellectual responses to the experience. The ability to trust our feelings becomes especially important as we try to distinguish between propaganda and art.

As Michael Arlen has pointed out in his book *Living Room War*, we have come to accept propaganda casually, as a daily fact of life, often without labeling it as such. It is difficult to find news today that is not propagandistic, for propaganda is simply the result of the ambience in which we exist. When we view a reported incident, what is important is not the actuality but the feelings surrounding it. Arlen suggests that propaganda has become so much a part of our lives that it is propaganda itself that has become reality.

One way we can help students develop the capacity to determine what is good and true and important in this ambience is to study specific films which demand that we decide for ourselves. These films should be studied in the light of the feelings they evoke rather than the facts they present. One of the most impressive propagandistic documentaries for this purpose is Leni Riefenstahl's *Triumph of the Will*, a paean to Hitler. It is also one of the most remarkable examples of the documentary as art. Certainly the factual film can be poetic, as documentaries like Flaherty's *Nanook of the North* or *Man of Aran* testify. Such films deserve special attention, for although we may set down rules and guidelines by the bookful, they are of little help when we confront a film freshly. In the classroom, the best training for distinguishing what is worth believing and what is spurious is not through indoctrination with rules of thumb or even by rigorous training in logical reasoning, though these may help at times, but by recognizing and examining one's own feelings in the light of other available information.

As an introduction, a study of commercials, the most available form of propaganda, is helpful. Here, some of the elementary forms of fallacy and cinematic manipulation can be introduced with a great deal of fun. The blatant and subtle appeals to sex and to fears about masculinity, power, youth, and so forth are interesting to study, but even more revealing is a study of our feelings about them. All of the commercials on television, no matter how obvious, appeal on a level of feeling, and sometimes that feeling may be difficult to recognize. Because commercials are short, extremely concise, and available for concentrated and enjoyable study, they serve as excellent preparation for more extensive study of how other films are essentially vehicles for evoking feeling.

The commercial mixes fact and fiction, and students often say that they don't really believe commercials the way they do documentaries. The documentary film and the fiction film are more similar than we usually realize, though, for documentaries contain a great range of expressive possibilities, from dry, academic canned lectures to some of the most powerfully experiential films available. A whole course can be developed around the question "What is a documentary film?" Ultimately, all films can be considered documentary in some sense; even the most subjective films may, for instance, be considered documentaries of states of consciousness.

It is often misleading to speak of realism versus fantasy in movies, as if documentaries were true and dispassionate and fiction films primarily fantastic and emotion-laden. Many films considered "realistic" rely heavily upon effects which give the appearance of realism and spontaneity, effects derived from the ability of the camera and the editor to distort time, space, and perspective and to juxtapose shots and sequences in order to present the illusion of reality. Conversely, fantasy in film relies on the concrete, physical details of the real world. It is not surprising, therefore, that some of the most outstanding documentary films are essentially poetic interpretations of physical reality.

One of the most famous examples is Robert Flaherty's *Nanook of the North*, which derives its appeal and power from its poetic rendition of practicality (see Fig. 19). As Bosley Crowther explains, before Flaherty the camera was conceived as a mechanism for recording aspects of the real world without any intention of creating illusions or fantasy. It was considered a device to look *at* rather than *into* its subject, and the films before Flaherty were much like today's typical travelogues. *Nanook*, the first major departure from this approach, is still one of the outstanding examples of how the documentary can reveal truth as well as fact. The distinction is often lost on students desensitized by TV news programs, and accustomed to accepting documentary film without questioning it either intellectually or emotionally.

Television exposes students to documentary films in one form

Figure 19. Nanook of the North.
Courtesy Pathe-Contemporary Films/McGraw-Hill

or another almost daily; many people, in fact, absorb most of their factual information from film, and many people in and out of government are alternately alarmed by and intrigued by the potential of film for persuasion. Probably the most dramatic evidence that documentary film can generate strong feelings is the claim that TV news coverage not only recorded but caused the riots of the 1968 Chicago Democratic convention.

The appeal of nonfiction is well known, for people are particularly receptive to something they accept as real. We see the appeal operate in the classroom when students become extraordinarily responsive to biography, or when they are so curious about how much of a fictional work, in print or on film, is based on the author's actual experience. Robert Flaherty's 1922 biographical documentary, though, is more than interesting because his treatment exposes the viewer to a human being whose particular kind of self-reliance, while initially unfamiliar, becomes intimately involving.

The involving quality of *Nanook* is a surprise for most students, who frequently anticipate a typically vapid travelogue about " 'way up north." Because students are conditioned by painful experience to dread films and lectures that pretend to "broaden horizons through exposure to customs of another land," the impact of *Nanook,* so refreshingly free from cliché, is quickly apparent. Some typical comments from students:

"It helps you see a little deeper than the normal fake movies."

"It is a film free from gimmickry."

"It showed you what it was intended to show without Hollywood's magic."

"You can *trust* this film."

It becomes apparent from comments like these that students are not concerned with the facts that Flaherty presented but with the feelings surrounding those facts. Furthermore, many of the comments are primarily responses to the general sense of honesty in Flaherty's film.

The absence of modern technological sophistication is deceptive. For example, the sequence in which *Nanook* builds an igloo in one hour is brilliantly concise, but it is far more than merely instructional, for the viewer realizes all the while the significance of the task—with less skill, Nanook and his family would perish. This becomes even more apparent later, when Nanook and his family struggle through a blizzard to an abandoned igloo. As Bosley Crowther points out, moreover, one of the reasons that the movie has retained its stature is its artistic structure; it is developed like a symphony.

Nanook himself makes this film so remarkably involving, for he is not merely a curiosity, a handy specimen, but a person. He is obviously aware of the camera in many sequences, and his tickled grin at the camera seems anything but a technical flaw; it is as genuine and memorable a communication as anyone could wish, a rarity in any film, documentary or not.

In some discussions, students may dismiss the stock response, "I learned a lot about how Eskimos live," to consider how the memorable details of the film affected them. Sometimes the most useful comments may be those which deride the film as primitive and irrelevant. The students whom the film does affect may offer suggestions which ask others to consider not how obviously different and remote from Nanook we are, but how much like him we are.

Still, those who demand more immediate social relevance from a film have a point. Flaherty's films, beautiful and impressive as they are, reveal a romantic vision of the noble primitive. We may legitimately ask what films like *Nanook* or *Man of Aran* have to do with the present issues of unjust hardship in America. It is perfectly understandable that Nanook is constantly on the verge of starving or freezing, for his environment is one of the most inhospitable on earth. But what about people who are starving today in our own land of hope, plenty, and opportunity?

When we select films with this issue in mind, we must consider more than social relevance; we must consider how the filmmaker has shaped his material. Two films which treat the issue of starvation in a land of plenty are the CBS Reports program *Harvest of Shame* and the later *Hunger in America*. Deliberately controversial, *Harvest of Shame* was presented on Thanksgiving evening and was a brutal reminder of the bleak condition of the migrant workers responsible for the meals gracing tables across the country. *Hunger in America*, too, spurred indignant protest that it was inappropriate, inaccurate, and disruptive. No strangers to propaganda, government officials protested *Hunger in America* on the grounds that the film was biased and that it neglected to give a fair hearing to the government's sincere efforts to help the victims. Whether these objections revealed a nitpicking disregard of the issue, the reaction showed once again that facts are often the vehicle for the real content of a film—feelings.

A film treating a contemporary controversy in the manner of Flaherty is *The Exiles*, written, directed, and produced by a group headed by Kent Mackenzie. It conveys the dilemma of the modern Indian, who is an anachronism caught between two cultures, alienated from his own people and land yet unable to gain acceptance in the white culture. The Indian has been attracting more attention lately, but *The Exiles* is the only film that intimately captures the desperation of the individuals themselves.

The film covers 14 hours in the lives of three young Indian men in Los Angeles. Life in the city is shown to be no better than the poverty-striken existence on the reservation, where conditions are no more appealing than Nanook's.

Like *Nanook, The Exiles* is a probing documentary of the everyday struggle of these Indians to survive in an indifferent or hostile land, and like Nanook himself, the Indians are not actors; they simply live their own story of attempting to escape despair by drinking, playing cards, picking up girls, fighting, and finally, on a hilltop high above the city, beating drums and singing tribal chants.

Figure 20. *The Anderson Platoon.*
Courtesy Pathe-Contemporary Films/McGraw-Hill

As Grierson explains, the principles of this kind of documentary are that the filmmaker masters his material on the spot, to achieve intimacy, and distinguishes between description and dramatization. He is not concerned solely with showing surface values but also with revealing the reality behind appearances. The camera is not merely a mechanism for "objectively" recording reality but is also an artist's instrument for creating a personal vision of it.[3]

Finally, Pierre Schoendorffer's *The Anderson Platoon*, one of the most rewarding documentaries to have appeared in the past few years, addresses the pervasive corrosive experience of our time—the Viet Nam War (see Fig. 20). The effectiveness of the film grows not from any political stand but from a sensitive rendition of day-to-day experiences of an American infantry platoon. By avoiding propaganda, unduly horrifying incidents and heroics, Schoendorffer communicates the drama of the personal experience of the war—the war behind the clichés.

Although black and white soldiers fight side by side, Schoendorffer doesn't dwell on racial issues. He avoids scoring easy trite points with the viewer. The war has numbed and raged and bewildered us for years and has been both dehumanized and dehumanizing in the mass media. *The Anderson Platoon*, however, conveys the personal experiences of the soldiers themselves, both as individuals and as a platoon. Moreover, Schoendorffer concentrates on the feelings of the soldiers about their total experiences, not simply on the strain of battle. He conveys, for instance, the loneliness of a soldier's leave in Saigon.

Schoendorffer has said that while making the film he "discovered America," adding that in Viet Nam he found the qualities of personal warmth and mutual respect epitomized in *The Anderson Platoon*. His explanation is unnecessary, though, for the film shows these qualities with intensity, and yet with restraint.

The number of excellent documentaries available for this kind of film study is astonishingly large. By examining the feelings surrounding these films, by recognizing and valuing intuition in discussion, and by relating intuitive comments to specific effects in the film, we can begin to see when and how film language becomes film rhetoric—a device to persuade by suggestion. Thus, this approach to studying documentaries sets the stage for helping

---

[3]Quoted in MacCann, R. D.: *A Montage of Theories*. New York: E. P. Dutton & Co., Inc., 1966, pp. 207-215.

students become a discerning audience, one which can *feel* as well as know how it sees.

BEFORE-AFTER EXERCISES

Asking a student simply to state his feelings may gain little result because students are so frequently unaware of their feelings. They need a set of opportunities to discover and acknowledge feelings in a supportive atmosphere. Before-after exercises are useful and nonthreatening. They involve dramatization, role-playing, discussion, and writing.

The use of a dramatic exercise to reveal the impact of a film upon our feelings or attitudes is often effective because the students are active. Ken Beattie of the University of Massachusetts developed one such exercise for Enrico's *An Occurrence at Owl Creek Bridge,* when he thought that a discussion of the film might not capture the empathy that students (in this case, college students) had with Farquhar.

Before showing the film, he divided the class into several sections, instructing them that they were all part of a chain of command which was to construct, justify, and carry out an order for executing a man strongly suspected of collusion with the enemy. They were to carry the order down the line from group to group until they had accomplished the task. As the class became involved in the exercise, there was much debate about whether they had sufficient evidence, whether execution might be delayed, and so forth. Finally the execution by hanging was dramatized; the exercise consumed about 30 minutes.

Then the group saw the film and was asked to repeat the exercise. The second time the exercise took only a few minutes. There was almost no questioning; everyone simply wanted to get it over with as quickly as possible. In discussing their feelings and behavior afterward, students acknowledged that they resisted going through the whole process again, but more importantly, they were also aware that they wanted to absolve themselves of any individual involvement or responsibility for the man's death. They simply followed orders. Ironically, their empathy with the condemned man in the film made them behave more impersonally.

A great many films may be treated with imaginative and revealing exercises like this one, simply by setting up a situation roughly paralleling that in the film. With teachers, for instance, I simulated a discipline problem, role-played it, showed *Corral,* and conducted role-playing again, comparing different feelings and behaviors in the light of the film. A similar exercise might illuminate the effects of *No Reason To Stay,* a widely used, humorous, but pointedly satirical short film about a boy who decides to drop out of school.

Another before-after exercise involves writing. Many visually exciting short films are difficult to talk about, and a discussion of the details of the film may lose momentum quickly. *Pigs!* is a good example of this problem. It is a delightful, thoroughly involving short about pigs, pigs, pigs in every size, assortment, and barnyard situation. We not only see pigs, we experience them in a tactile way as they trundle through a field of flowers, wallow mudlusciously, snort, squeal, snuffle, and grunt.

Figure 21. Children Adrift.
Courtesy Pathe-Contemporary Films/McGraw-Hill

Figure 22. *The Responsive Eye.*
Courtesy Pathe-Contemporary Films/McGraw-Hill

The tactile quality of this film is hard to catch in words, but words can demonstrate how the film affected an audience. Write the word "pigs" on the board and have students jot down figurative language, free associations, and details for a few minutes as they think about pigs; repeat the exercise after the film and compare results. Invariably the second exercise will reveal a greater range of association and detail, and fewer stereotypes and clichés.

Variations on this exercise can be conducted with countless other films which evoke strong feelings but defy discussion. The object of such exercises is not only to sharpen observation of detail, but also to reveal the differences in feelings as a result of seeing the film. At the same time, naturally, these writing exercises can provide practice in approaches to sound composition, such as comparison, contrast, emphasis, and point of view, but

Figure 23. *Help! My Snowman's Burning.*
Courtesy Pathe-Contemporary Films/McGraw-Hill

teaching these techniques should not be the sole reason for using the exercise. Eventually, a subtle visual narrative like *Children Adrift*, a visually stunning film, and like *Allures* or *The Responsive Eye*, or even heavily symbolic, humorous films like *Time Piece* or *Help! My Snowman's Burning* can become richer experiences when accompanied by this exercise.

AN EXERCISE IN VALUE CLARIFICATION: THE VALUE CONTINUUM

The value continuum is only one of several techniques for clarifying values; I recommend that you read *Values and Teaching*, by Raths, Harmin, and Simon (see Appendix II) for a full explanation of the many resources in value clarification. Films are particularly rich sources of material for value clarification because they stimulate feelings as well as thoughts, and because through drama they comfort the student with values in action. A film like *The Exiles* has many implications for values, and the uproar created by *Hunger in America* occurred primarily because the film challenged the value system of our government. *Toys*, a powerful short which depicts a miniature fantasy war among plastic war toys, as seen through the eyes of children, allegedly prompted a toy manufacturer to curtail its production of war toys (see Fig. 24).

The value continuum is based on a central tenet of value theory: to hold a value one must choose it publicly and freely from a set of alternatives. The value continuum exposes a full range of

Figure 24. Toys.
Courtesy Pathe-Contemporary Films/McGraw-Hill

possible alternatives. One is that when an issue is identified, state two polar positions. For example, on the issue of pollution one position might be that pollution should be uncontrolled in order to foster free enterprise and an expanding industrial society; an opposite position would be that pollution should be stringently controlled in the public interest. These two positions should be stated as extremely as possible. The task of the class is to identify other positions on the issue, placing them on the continuum.

To illustrate, on one end of the continuum sits Polluting Paul, who actually goes out of his way to pollute. He campaigns against legislation for clean air, writes to his congressman to defeat antipollution bills, and deliberately litters. On the other end of the continuum sits Clean Clara, who not only contributes all of her allowance and free time to antipollution campaigns, but scrubs the coins first with biodegradable soap. In the middle sits Compromising Connie, who verbally supports antipollution campaigns but has not written to her congressman; she uses a litterbag in her car but does not use lead-free gasoline because she doesn't have the right credit card. Other students then may place themselves on the continuum in relation to these positions, explaining their choices, and suggest other alternatives.

Students may repeat this exercise after seeing a film that raises the issue, explaining why they have or have not changed their stand. For example, the exercise might be used to examine discipline in *Corral;* or the limits of patriotism before and after watching *Point of Order!*, a record of the McCarthy Army hearings; or war, after seeing *Toys, Neighbors,* or *The Battle of Culloden.*[4]

Raths, Harmin, and Simon describe 21 value-clarifying strategies, most of which have obvious applications to film study. They are particularly useful for exploring the effect of a film upon students because they ask the student to explore his thoughts and feelings further and to consider acting on them.

AN EXERCISE IN FEEDBACK

Sometimes, if you wish to elicit feedback on your own behavior, you may use a film which clearly applies to the classroom situation. *No Reason To Stay, Corral, Boundary Lines, High School, The Critic,* and *The Student* are examples.

---

[4]For an extensive list of films about war, see the December, 1967, issue of *Media and Methods.*

Prior to this exercise you must first create an atmosphere unequivocally free of threats of reprisal. Even the most confident teacher may receive some surprising feedback, and you should not invite it unless you are willing to accept it and to consider acting on it. The exercise itself is simple: invite comparisons between what students felt about various sections of the film and what they feel in the class itself, being specific whenever possible.

Before using this exercise, train students in giving feedback. That is, in order for feedback to be useful rather than merely critical, it should be descriptive rather than evaluative. For example, a student might point out similarities between the situation in *No Reason To Stay* and his own school or classroom, stating how he feels in each situation. Then you can negotiate about possible change without being defensive.

For example, perhaps a student resents having to live by the bell. There is little anyone may be able to do about bells in the school, but perhaps further feedback may reveal that the students sometimes feel that you prolong discussions or writing exercises unnecessarily in order to kill time before the bell. Or perhaps you have developed certain stereotyped teaching behaviors that have negative effects on the students. Of course, the students may ask you for feedback about their own behavior, an ideal opportunity for you to examine behavior without being authoritarian. Thus, feedback exercises related to the film are a useful way to develop a climate of freedom in the classroom and can be a major step for increasing student participation in the management of classroom activities.

EXERCISES IN COMPARING AND CONTRASTING FILMS

A common procedure in all classes, comparing and contrasting can be well applied to film study, but with a difference. In film study, comparing and contrasting should treat the feelings and intuitions of the audience as well as the elements and thematic implications of the movie.

David Sohn and Hart Leavitt, whose book *Stop, Look, and Write!* is designed for teaching composition through the study of photographs, explain one of the most important principles for comparing and contrasting pictures. It is neither interesting nor useful to compare or contrast what is obvious, they say; instead, we should try to point out what is *not* obvious, by revealing differences within similarities, and vice versa.

Figure 25. *Cattle Ranch.*
Courtesy Pathe-Contemporary Films/McGraw-Hill

Although this approach at first glance seems designed to teach specific writing skills, Sohn and Leavitt stress that the basic objective is to train students how to see. Composition is not an end in itself, then, but simply one expression of the student's ability to see perceptively. Filmmaking would be an equally legitimate expression of that ability; so would discussion.

Using this principle, Paul Carrico developed an exercise in comparing and contrasting *Cattle Ranch, Corral,* and *Dream of the Wild Horses.* Although the subject matter of these films may be roughly similar, the three cinematic treatments are different in many ways. Studying those differences and similarities is a good introduction to several major elements in cinematic expression— rhythm, pace, color, composition, and sound. Now, the appearance of *Tamer of Wild Horses* extends the possibilities of this exercise further and introduces another element — animation.

A similar exercise might be conducted with two films about trains, *Pacific 231* and *Castro Street,* and of course the possibilities in a given genre, such as the western, are virtually inexhaustible. Ultimately, the process of comparing and contrasting the films and their effects on the audience may lead to a concentrated study of the styles of different directors — the heart of advanced film study.

STUDYING ELEMENTS OF CINEMATIC EXPRESSION

An increasingly widespread approach to film study concentrates on specific elements of film, including the analysis of shots, scenes, and sequences, and the study of composition, rhythm, pace, lighting, color, tempo, and symbolism. This approach is especially useful in helping students to become thoroughly familiar with *how* to watch movies, and it has the additional virtue of being nonevaluative. Kuhns and Stanley's *Exploring the Film* uses this general approach to film study, and many other books are available for studying each element extensively (e.g., Huss and Silverstein's *The Film Experience*; see Appendix I).

Consequently, I will not dwell on this method but will indicate a corollary approach to studying nonliterary aspects of movies — isolating compositional elements. For instance, directors often use spatial and architectural relationships to indicate human relationships or psychological conditions. As Raymond Durgnat has pointed out in *Films and Feelings,* architecture has been the expressive vehicle for pathos, alienation, lyrical realism, and metaphor in movies for decades. As he put it, "A fundamental equation in cinema is that landscape = state of soul."

The major reasons for isolating various elements for study are to equip students with a vocabulary and conceptual framework for discussing, writing about, and making films, and to encourage them to think of movies in totally nonliterary ways. Thus, it is frequently useful to think of film as if it were more closely related to dance, painting, music, sculpture, and architecture than to theater and the novel. Finally, isolating elements of film is designed to sensitize students to the ways in which a director orchestrates all the details of his material, often intuitively but always deliberately, to communicate a particular vision of experience.

STOPPING A FILM

This procedure, one of the well-known tricks of the trade, often appears to be little more than an irritating device to con students into discussion. As some students have complained, they feel tense after a film has been running for a while because they keep wondering when the teacher is going to flick the switch.

The problem with this technique occurs when the emphasis is on talking about plot or theme rather than the images. For this reason, students should see a film in its entirety first, so that there is no sense of a guessing game, a mere rehashing of plot, or an excursion into character analysis for its own sake. Stopping a film the second or third time through can, however, help students become aware of cinematic tensions which comprise a rich film experience.

The focus of discussion should be upon the filmmaker's way of creating and resolving these cinematic tensions to create the film's structure, and the effect of these tensions and resolutions upon the audience. Thus, when the film resumes, students will be more observant of the particular ways in which the director resolved a given problem, and much more aware of how the movie expresses the director's personal artistic vision.

If the school is fortunate enough to have a projector which can freeze the frame (e.g., the Bell & Howell model 552) the students may have an image before them during discussion and will be able to refer to specific compositional elements in the image. Thus, they can discuss the way the director is at that moment using spatial relationships or architecture to express human relationships.

This exercise is also useful in preparing students for their own filmmaking. Student filmmaking is so often a haphazard affair at first because they have trouble defining for themselves a particular artistic problem. Consequently their first films are often inconsistent and cliché-ridden. Other students, reduced to saying whether they like the efforts or not, or giving suggestions about what they would have done, have trouble providing constructive remarks. Isolating and specifying artistic problems and investigating in thorough detail alternative ways of solving those problems give students a framework for working purposefully.

EXPERIMENTING WITH SOUND

We are so used to thinking of movies as a visual experience that we often neglect the importance of the soundtrack. Simply show a film without sound (e.g., *Pacific 231,* a *tour de force* in editing) and you can demonstrate how strongly sound affects the images themselves. Some exercises in manipulating and studying soundtracks often highlight this crucial dimension of movies. I have already mentioned the way this exercise can illuminate the experience of seeing *The Critic*; many short films, particularly those of Pathe-Contemporary (c/o McGraw-Hill), contain few if any words, and are therefore useful for experimenting with different soundtracks.

The exercise is particularly instructive, too, for student film-makers. For example, one student made a film which concentrated on the ways light played on water, and he constructed six sound tracks—electronic music which he composed on a Moog synthesizer, a Bach fugue, recorded selections from Debussy and MacDowell, commercial "mood" music, contemporary rock, and a mixture of various sounds—to create six completely different film experiences. One intriguing discovery was that whatever music or sounds he used tended automatically to fit the rhythm of the images on the screen.

Tony Schwartz, an expert in audiotape technology, has demonstrated both on recordings and at New York film conferences that working with sound has inexhaustible possibilities and creates infinite surprises. In fact, study of sound and the production of audiotapes can overwhelm some student films. No matter, the same principles apply to the study of sound, for sound is also intimately related to feeling. Students may choose, in fact, to develop autiotapes as a way of expressing their feelings and ideas.

MULTI-MEDIA AND MULTI-SCREEN
APPROACHES

In the past few years, students have become increasingly interested in multi-screen and multi-media presentations, partly because light shows have been in vogue, partly because they are simply fun to watch. Eventually, though, light shows become tiresome and students would like to do more than play with flashing lights and loud rock music; they would like to communicate something more. Fortunately, they can when they selectively experiment with sound montage and slide-tape presentations together with film, pantomime, dance, pageantry, and drama.

Thomas Andrews, who teaches film and drama at the Kent School, developed an excellent example of effectively coordinated multi-media, which illustrates how multi-media and multi-screen approaches extend the principles of the image-sound skim. On three screens he showed *Dream of the Wild Horses*, *Sky*, and a portion of *N.Y., N.Y.*, together with an audiotape which contained, among other things, evocations of the King and Kennedy assassinations. The interplay among the scenes and soundtrack provoked a great deal of discussion about the different ways people perceived the presentation. Because there is so much material present, spectators view it selectively. Later, as they exchange comments about what they saw and felt, they experience the basic spirit of all good film discussions.

The comments that I heard about his particular presentation were especially revealing. One spectator concentrated upon the interplay between *Dream of the Wild Horses* and *Sky* to the point of resisting the more frenzied, distorted images in *N.Y., N.Y.*, until the assassination references on the soundtrack suddenly pulled him to the urban images of *N.Y., N.Y.* Did he automatically associate violence with cities? He could not be sure, but he cannot stand cities, and New York makes him tense and a bit fearful. Another viewer felt irritated as he experienced difficulty in concentrating on any screen. He constantly tried to fit the images into a visual commentary and felt compelled to invent ingenious connections, whether they legitimately existed or not. He noted that in class he tended to insist on structure, and the notion of nondirective teaching of film appalled him. He wondered whether there was any way to reach students who felt comfortable in chaotic situations like the one he had just experienced, but he also said that he would further examine possibilities in film study for alternative solutions that might appeal to such students. Still another spectator found a way to enjoy the presentation by looking not at the images as content, but at the patterns and rhythms of color and composition on the screens.

Finally, because the images and sounds can be carefully controlled in a slide-tape presentation, they are particularly rich resources for preparing students to make their own films. A student can use a slide-tape show to accompany a short film, determining fairly precisely what he wants to achieve, and later, in discussion, examine what he has actually communicated to his audience.

THE FISHBOWL

A device for examining the different ways that members of an audience see involves a popular small group procedure called the fishbowl. One group sits in a circle and discusses a topic while another small group observes silently outside the circle. The two groups can then reverse roles, or the observers can comment on what has occurred in the inner circle. In one variation of the procedure, a chair in the inner circle may be left vacant and outsiders may temporarily join the inner circle in order to contribute an important comment.

A particularly revealing way to use this technique is with two different types of groups — e.g., representatives from two different kinds of classes, two different age groups, boys and girls, or students from different shools. Frequently this variation helps groups become aware of how the context in which they see a film affects the way they see it.

The procedure is useful, too, in encouraging participation. Because the group outside the circle is not supposed to participate but to observe, members often store up an enormous number of ideas and observations, particularly during an image-sound skim. When they finally get their chance to participate, some students are nearly ready to explode.

Finally, the fishbowl technique is useful for observing group process, which is its original purpose. Students are used to being in classes all day, but they are often unaware of what is actually happening in discussion and see no way to change the patterns of interaction because they have not analyzed them. Observers of the fishbowl can chart the patterns of interaction — who talks, who asks questions, who interrupts, who asks for clarification, who gives answers, who builds on previous comments, who initiates ideas — and later give the inner group feedback for further discussion. The fishbowl, then, is another device to encourage collaborative participation in creating a desirable classroom climate.

I have said a great about collaboration, the need for teachers to develop a partnership with students in a variety of ways. To develop this kind of climate may seem impossible, given the reward system presently dominating most schools. However, within a film study class a teacher can begin to organize interaction around different values such as seeing, feeling, listening, and questioning, rather than around encouraging students to come up with "right" answers for higher grades. This entails organizing a class on different objectives, and planning for change, the subject of the next chapter.

5

"YES, BUT!"

How many times have you heard that phrase? It's a powerful reply. Someone has said that it takes at least three "attaboys" to equal one "Yes, but," and if you are interested in humanistic approaches to education, including film study, you had better start warming up your attaboys. This chapter is a set of attaboys to start you on your way.

The first "yes, but" is the prevailing trend toward behavioral objectives in curriculum development and teaching. I do not propose rejecting behavioral objectives entirely; rather, I suggest using them selectively and supplementing them with what Elliott Eisner has called expressive objectives (see Appendix II).

BEHAVIORAL OBJECTIVES

Robert Mager points out that behavioral objectives are designed to answer three reasonable questions:

1. What is it that we must teach?
2. How will we know when we have taught it?
3. What materials and procedures will work best to teach what we want to teach?[1]

When teaching, we often state objectives poorly; we do not know why or where we are headed because our goals are vague. We talk about "knowing" material, "understanding" concepts, and "learning," yet we often cannot evaluate learning by measuring change in behavior according to the goals we originally selected. Behavioral objectives require that we define learning by identifying activities displayed by the learner, and that when evaluating our teaching and the students' learning we use specific criteria for terminal behavior.

Behavioral objectives have contributed a great deal toward making proposed practices rational and explicit, and they have

---

[1] Mager, R. F.: *Preparing Instructional Objectives.* Palo Alto: Fearon Publishers, 1962, p. v.

helped us to think analytically about both the means and the ends of education. Based on a systematic analysis of learning in terms of measurable outcomes, behavioral objectives have some obvious applications to some features of film education—for example, teaching basic elements of cinematic communication, principles of filmmaking, principles of film criticism, principles of comparing and contrasting films, and ways to use movies to illuminate the content of printed material and prescribed discussion topics.

BEYOND BEHAVIORISM TO EXPRESSIVE OBJECTIVES

However, as Eisner stresses, this exclusively rational approach ignores covert, experiential, unmeasurable aspects of life and hence neglects significant aspects of personal meaning. Moreover, because this approach rejects objectives which cannot be specified behaviorally, it homogenizes learning activities, sets up common expectations for students with different backgrounds, leads to educational practices which assume that educationally significant ends are specifiable in advance, and disregards possibilities for student participation in curriculum design.

Clearly, these drawbacks critically affect the major aims I have been advocating for film education. Not only do the nonlinear, irrational aspects of cinematic expression and the psychology of audience response resist this kind of categorization, but the learning that occurs in film discussions, though often measurable, is by definition impossible to specify beforehand. Finally, for the the teacher as well as the student, surprise is the source of learning in film discussions and in filmmaking.

By contrast, an expressive objective does not specify what behavior the student is to acquire but instead describes an educational encounter. An expressive objective identifies the situation in which students are to work, the problem they are to confront, and the task they are to perform, but *not* what they are to learn. Eisner explains that because expressive objectives invite students to explore and to focus on issues of particular interest to the learner, the products of their learning are as diverse as the learners themselves, and "the task is not to apply a common standard, but to reflect on what has been produced or shared, to illuminate its uniqueness and significance."

Expressive objectives are a way to organize our thinking about what processes of learning and growth we want to foster using film in the classroom. These objectives enable us to support expression and examination of feeling and intuition as well as analytical thinking. Despite the contributions of behavioral approaches, then, we need to balance them with humanistic objectives. Alexander Lowen[2] articulates the need this way: "Of the two ingredients in behavior, feeling is more important than knowledge. But our whole educational system is geared to knowledge and the denial of feeling. My argument is that . . . knowledge divorced from feeling is empty and meaningless. An education that is to be effective in preparing a child for life must take into account his emotional as well as his mental development."

The basic difference between the strictly behavioral approach to learning and the humanistic approach is that behaviorists believe that teaching causes learning, while humanistic educators believe that we cause our own learning; it does not happen *to* us; it is not caused by others. The approaches I have described grow from the humanistic premise that the process of exploring a film should concentrate on creating possibilities for discovering and sharing personal meanings rather than on acquiring specific knowledge.

Clearly, film education can become more than a useful innovation for enlivening classrooms. It is a potentially powerful catalyst for creating greater freedom in schools by fostering humanistic aims and practices. Movies are occasions for educational encounters which carry many opportunities for building emotional as well as intellectual bridges between individuals and groups. David Mallery has shown, for instance, how film can become an important ingredient in the life of an entire school (see Appendix I).

One potential outgrowth of film education, already evident in several independent schools, is the interdisciplinary use of movies. By bringing classrooms together with a movie, teachers and students can regularly experience some of the exciting cross-fertilization of ideas and perspectives which occurs when people explore an intense experience from different standpoints.

For instance, Ethel Booth, a teacher at Beverly Hills High School, organized a film and videotape discussion under a grant from the American Film Institute, in which she demonstrated how an involving movie can stimulate honest, lively communication among students from different schools and different economic and social backgrounds. Groups composed of white Beverly High

---

[2]Alexander Lowen is a psychotherapist practicing in New York City. He has written several books and is the major proponent of bioenergetic therapy.

students and black students from Crenshaw High School in Los Angeles separately discussed *The Heart Is a Lonely Hunter,* exchanged videotapes of their discussions, and then joined to share feelings, impressions, and ideas.

Ethel Booth began with separate groups on the premise that (a) people reveal themselves more freely when they are talking not about themselves, but about a film and (b) people talk more freely in a group of people similar to themselves in social, educational, and economic background, and should therefore have this kind of experience before encountering more complex discussions.

Videotaping the discussions was a particularly effective device, since videotape captured a great deal that might otherwise have been lost to any but the participants themselves. In addition, the experiment made it possible for each participant to examine the reactions of others in his group, his own responses, and those of the other group.

Although this project required much time, effort, planning, and cooperation, and about 700 dollars, it demonstrates the potential of movies in eroding some major educational barriers. A teacher needn't begin so ambitiously, though. He can make significant strides within his own school by inviting a variety of groups to discuss movies together.

It is now not unusual to combine English and social studies classes for various reasons. Combined science and humanities classes are also rewarding. The students, naturally, are not specialists in the field they are studying at a given time of day; they are simply in one course rather than another at that moment because of an accident of the schedule. However, the ways in which they experience the movie and relate to the different teachers present—and the way the teachers respond to one another—reveal a great deal about how they view themselves and others.

In such classes the teachers of the sciences, committed as they may be to behavioral objectives, directly experience the rewards of expressive objectives. As they become involved in the encounters, they often begin to see their own students, their colleagues, and themselves in fresh ways. It is also worth their while to pursue the implications of such experiences, for the most creative intellectual activities, especially in scientific research, are organized around expressive objectives. The most productive researchers and inventors, after all, operate on educated guesses and shrewd hunches, and are most interested in exposing fresh, feasible alternatives. Their thinking process is more often intuitive than strictly analytical.[3]

Jerome Bruner has pointed out that we neglect intuitive thinking in schools. Intuitive thinking, or coming to conclusions on the basis of less than full evidence, is important, he says, because we rarely *have* all the evidence we need to be certain. Shrewd, educated guesses are all we usually have in most cases. We should take advantage of all the chances we can to develop students' capacities to trust their intuitive thinking and develop attractive possibilities. Bruner puts it very strongly: "A teacher who says, 'you're only guessing,' should be tried as an educational criminal."

A TOTAL SYSTEM

Talk of educational criminals, though popular and often justified, does little to help us improve the educational life of a school. As Mallery remarks, however, although there is a great deal of "we vs. them" talk in schools these days, it seems to be diminishing in some quarters, especially among teachers using movies.

The "we vs. them" opposition constantly afflicting schools is often most apparent between administrators and everyone else because administrators are usually most removed from the life of the school and are viewed as judges and master disciplinarians. What better way to help them share in the life of the school than by inviting them to participate as equals in a film discussion? Independent schools have reported gratifying successes in developing significant personal communication among teachers, students, and administrators, and many report that the effects carried over to other situations as well. Although public school administrators usually have little time to spare, some may be willing to reexamine their priorities and join a discussion. If they do, they may find that some of their headaches cure themselves.

Some of the most involving and surprising film discussions occur when younger students join older students, and the greater the age gap, the better. The most appealing aspect of these discussions is that older students rarely put down younger students. In addition, everyone immediately senses that the discussion will move best if they concentrate on visual elements and feelings rather than abstract ideas. Moreover, combining younger and older

---

[3]See Polanyi, Michael: *Personal Knowledge.* New York: Harper and Row, Publishers, 1964.

students is one of the best ways to acquaint both groups with the spirit behind the approaches I have been describing.

Although I have recommended a variety of procedures for film education, I have granted equal time to a plea for humanistic education. It is entirely possible, though, that a humanistic approach may seem unrealistic and threatening for the teachers who would have to alter their comfortable behavioral patterns, relinquish heavy emotional investments, and possibly initially face opposition from both students and teachers. We know, for instance, that students frequently become unsettled—even openly hostile—to unexpected democratic situations, and that learning to use freedom and develop trust takes time.

Does this mean that my approaches to film education do not apply to these teachers, or that film education should avoid these teachers if it is to survive? Not necessarily. Pauline Kael may be right, but only if in promoting film education you neglect to design and implement strategies of systematic planning for change.

CHANGE

Planning for change with film education must be a thoughtful, painstaking process because it involves asking people to alter their objectives, attitudes, and classroom behavior—in short, their personal and professional values. In addition, you are asking them to help you alter institutional values. Without these changes, the introduction of movies into the curriculum may be nearly meaningless—tantamount to lip service. Without question, the selection of materials, procedures, and methods of evaluating classroom activities is not so much a question of techniques as it is an issue of values.

My recommendations for film education may seem less like procedures than idealized and perhaps unreachable objectives. Given the conventional rewards of our educational system, with their emphasis on grades, competition, and dependency upon the teacher, it is unlikely that any but those rare, naturally humanistic teachers can adopt and build upon my suggestions from scratch.

Of course, I am not suggesting that you be able to breeze into class one bright day, show a film, state a few new ground rules, and begin a discussion where kids no longer compete or put each other down, where they listen sensitively and accurately, where they share feelings openly, and where they comment without fear of the teacher's judgment. Certainly such a class is ideal, and even experienced encounter groups take a long time to reach that point, if they ever do. However, a teacher can begin to move toward that state of affairs faster than he expects by thinking of himself as a facilitator of change both inside and outside the classroom.

Despite the recent ferment about film and film study, the heady brew of possibilities is likely to go flat without systematic planning for change. Therefore you must start not by trying to introduce film education right away or by expanding your program immediately, but by planning for change—fostering a climate in which film education, or perhaps some other appropriate kind of program, can gain acceptance and continue to grow.

In order to facilitate change, you must adopt three roles: those of a catalyst, a solution giver, and a process helper. You must be a catalyst in order to overcome inertia in your school or system; you must start things moving. You must be a solution-giver by providing resources and helping to develop a range of alternatives at the appropriate time for receptive people who would like to promote change but cannot see how to do it. Above all, you must be a process helper, a person who assists other faculty, students, and administrators in determining *how* to change.

Ronald Havelock, at the Institute for Social Research at the University of Michigan, has shown that the process helper can provide valuable assistance in showing others

1. How to recognize and define needs. . . .
2. How to diagnose problems and set objectives. . . .
3. How to acquire relevant resources. . . .
4. How to select or create solutions. . . .
5. How to adapt and install solutions. . . .
6. How to evaluate solutions to determine if they are satisfying his needs.[4]

Havelock further points out that an insider can be an effective change agent because he is familiar with the system, feels its problems deeply, and is a familiar face, a "known quantity." Sometimes a change agent must be an insider; this seems especially true in film education, where so much depends on the ability of the classroom teacher to create a climate where film can stay alive. However, an insider cannot succeed by working alone. Because most research studies show that change depends most heavily on the administrator, who sets tone, opens doors, and provides psychological and material support, it is crucial to involve him from the beginning.

---

[4]Havelock, Ronald G.: *A Guide to Innovation in Education.* Ann Arbor: Institute for Social Research, The University of Michigan, 1970, p. 7.

There must be full involvement of administrators, parents, students, curriculum committees, department heads, and any others who would be affected by the change or who can influence it. That is, the approach to developing film and humanistic education must be as collaborative as possible. This may mean negotiating many compromises along the way, achieving consensus wherever feasible. In film education, for instance, many teachers will probably want to teach movies as if they were literature—all my arguments aside—and some enthusiastic supporters of film may become enemies if their pet theories of film criticism or preferences about particular movies fail to receive a full hearing. Nevertheless, self-sustaining change may be impossible without these people. Emphasis must be on providing several alternatives; if some turn out to be more successful than others with students, they may eventually serve as models for further change.

If you intend to begin specific changes in your classroom or school, you will probably encounter many obstacles—obstacles which can defeat you if you insist on only one way to innovate.

For instance, in diagnosing the problem, you may discover that film education may not in fact solve the actual problem existing in your school. If you persistently advocate film education and if your experiments do not live up to the advertising, film may die of neglect, be rejected entirely, or become an isolated adjunct to the regular curriculum.

ALWAYS HAVE ALTERNATIVES

Acquiring relevant resources in film education is necessary if you are to avoid a narrow approach to innovation (see Appendices for resources), but even the most outstanding resources in film education may be insufficient data for choosing a solution. Film education, after all, is not a panacea, nor is it necessarily appropriate. In practice, it may actually fail to address problems it seems designed to solve, because other factors may be operating. For example, some students may feel an urgent need to see concrete, daily evidence of learning, and may resist film or open discussions. Kenneth Clark, a behavioral psychologist, convinced the city of Washington, D.C., to adapt his program for exactly that reason: students in urban schools, he contends, need to learn basic skills, especially reading, first and foremost. Some teachers may have discipline problems which film will only exacerbate. Still other teachers or students may be so unaccustomed to anything remotely resembling the discussions I have described that those procedures would only invite confusion, if not total chaos.

Perhaps film study should enter gradually in some situations, or only after teachers have experimented and succeeded with alternative methods of classroom management. Perhaps it should begin on a pilot basis, with a few especially interested teachers. Perhaps it should develop through a film club. Or perhaps film education is not, after all, a valid solution to a given problem and would probably not gain acceptance. In this case the advocate should save his material for another time, perhaps another place.

Almost as soon as film study begins, the model must undergo revision in order to meet special considerations, often characteristics of the system. Workshops for in-service teacher training may be necessary before teachers can use fresh approaches to discussion. Team teaching strategies may be desirable in order to help traditional teachers experiment comfortably with new behaviors. Some film programs may have to be revised to accommodate the schedule or demands of an overcrowded curriculum for the time being. Several teachers in a department may feel a need for detailed study guides, lesson plans, and writing assignments for their classes, and they may wish to design certain common reasonable questions that all students seeing a given film should explore both in discussion and in writing. Some may contend, correctly, that such approaches will legitimize film study in the minds of some skeptical teachers and administrators, not to mention parents and students who resist any situation where grades are not clearly at stake.

Legitimizing an approach or program does not necessarily entail altering it beyond recognition. Often the concession simply involves establishing further alternatives, providing more choices. Thus, perhaps it may be impossible to eliminate grades in film study, and some teachers may insist on assigning major essays at the end of a unit, but you may use your own innovative grading procedure to meet this requirement, perhaps by forming individual contracts with your students or having the students grade themselves. You must realize, though, that if your special way of circumventing the system is likely to make waves, you must nurture your innovation separately and systematically, or you may jeopardize the larger program you have worked so hard to create. Choose your battles wisely.

The central feature of all the developmental stages of innovation is full involvement of those who can promote or hinder it, especially the system's gatekeepers: administrators, curriculum committees, department heads, and influential people like Mr. Gradgrind. Unless they feel a sense of ownership and consensus about the proposed practices, the innovation is unlikely to become stabilized. Furthermore, its maintenance will depend too heavily on its original advocates. For this reason, you must facilitate developing other change agents around you—people who can create and maintain strategies for self-renewing change.

In film education this means that a group of teachers, administrators, and students, if possible, constantly redesign film programs, stimulating continuing research into ways to improve them and making certain that they are meeting changing needs.

This summary is an extremely sketchy outline of the change process, designed only to identify some major issues which you should face. Typically, teachers interested in movies want to do more than stimulate their own classes; they want to stimulate larger changes. Even if they begin, as I did, with relatively provincial motives, they cannot ignore the possibilities. Film is simply too rich and exciting and liberating when used well. Any teacher who has glimpsed that bright world of personal freedom, excitement, honesty, and discovery outside his cave cannot be reclaimed, and it is no wonder that some advocates seem annoyingly messianic about film.

Proselytizing, though, even on a large scale such as a regional film conference, is not enough. Neither is marshaling all the soundest arguments to confront administrators, skeptics, and opponents—all the arguments to counter the external "Yes, *but!*" The film educator must become more than a teacher who loves to use movies in his own classes, who wants them in the curriculum so that everyone can enjoy them, and who wants other teachers to join the movement. He must become a change agent, a person concerned with helping process rather than promoting causes.

Film may indeed be a foot in the door leading to humanistic, process education, but the door is barely open a crack. Curricula that deal directly with feelings about identity, connectedness, and potency; curricula organized around value clarification; plans for open campuses; schools without walls; and schools organized around collaborative curriculum design are other approaches with the same general aim. Indeed, in the light of these possibilities, this book has a limited perspective in that it treats film primarily as a classroom activity. Since classrooms, tight schedules, crowded curricula, and traditionally trained teachers are likely to be with us for some time to come, we must organize film study around these constraints. At the same time, however, we must work toward removing those constraints and securing more options in the design of educational experiences. In fact, it is educational redesign which must be our basic concern.

There are several compelling reasons why you should think about redesign, whatever your official status in the system. Film alone cannot meet the critical problems in American education, problems which can overwhelm it as they have other promising innovations. Taken alone, teaching with movies is simply one more example of the Band-Aid approach to education. Results of surveys of E.S.E.A. Title III, which is devoted to promoting innovation, have shown that the programs have had minimal effect on education. Evidently both the organization and the people in it must change before they will even accept innovations, much less allow them to flourish and multiply.

If film education is not to be just one more desert flower, it must have planned support. Embarking on a project to change a school in a big way may seem like an enormous, perhaps impossible task to any teacher, and perhaps you are just interested for the time being in using movies to stimulate classes and perhaps experiment with new teaching methods in a relatively small way. However, I contend that all those procedures and methods amount to little more than fleeting sparks of life in the classroom, as evanescent as a movie itself, without a determined effort toward substantial change. Even workshops for individual teachers who want to try facilitating may fail, for while individuals may change, little effect will occur in the education of the students unless organizations change in a manner to support the new behavior of the faculty. The pressures to "adjust" to the system are simply overwhelming.

There is, though, hope for the individual or the group that seriously wants to promote change. One promising strategy is to build reference groups inside and outside the system, devoted not only to supporting individuals who wish to innovate but also to promoting change within the organization. Everyone, of course, knows a few kindred souls on the faculty, but few take advantage of other resources in the community—parents, university faculty, teachers in other schools, ministers, and others. A strong support group working systematically for sound innovation and involving the people affected by potential change can succeed. Recent research[5] shows, in fact, that teachers can thrive with this kind of support and can influence others to become venturesome. Building such a group is the subject of the final chapter.

---

[5]Cooperative Educational Research Laboratory, Inc.: *Conceptual Base of Program I: Specialist in Continuing Education.* (Consultants; assessment), Division of Educational Laboratories, Bureau of Research, United States Office of Education, Department of Health, Education and Welfare, Washington, D.C. Contract # OE C-3-7-061391-3061, July, 1969.

6

A LITTLE HELP FROM MY FRIENDS

Do you want to change your school but feel that your hands are tied? Undoubtedly you have entertained many good innovative ideas which have been lost along the way, killed, or isolated like a tumor in your own classroom. You may be skeptical about film education, despite its promise, because you have seen other potentially exciting programs meet a sorry fate. Conversation in the teachers' lounge has degenerated into gripe sessions. You are under constant pressure to maintain control, cover the material, and perhaps adjust to a new job. Reading publications that dangle all sorts of exciting ideas in front of you adds to your frustrations; all you can do is dream about the things you would love to try in your classroom.

Have you also sensed kindred souls around you but have had trouble getting together with them? Sometimes they are to be found in other buildings or school systems and, often, not even in the field of education.

SMALL SUPPORT GROUPS

Here is a plan for organizing a small support reference group, one of the best resources for teachers who are not satisfied with the educational system and want to change it. You can eliminate fragmented, piecemeal change efforts. You will meet a deep human need to work intimately with supportive people. The plan is simple and practical — something you can *do*, not just read about.

Both you and your school will benefit from participating in a small support group. Group meetings themselves prove especially meaningful because of the opportunity to share ideas, support, and encouragement. Research shows that members become more personally involved with their teaching, more effective and less talkative communicators, more student-centered, more open to new methods. Furthermore, we have already seen such small groups change the life of a whole school.

Small groups of teachers in a midwestern city began to assess themselves, solicit feedback from their classes, and invent workable plans to improve the experiences of children. The principal of one building got involved; he invited feedback on how he was coming across to his building staff and how well he was achieving his purposes. His teachers then worked with him to establish close collaborative working relationships. New teachers hired for the coming year were included in the program. The staff was so enthusiastic and encouraged by their progress that they expressed regret that a summer vacation would prevent them from immediately launching their plans for fall.

The staff of another school in rural Saskatchewan began meeting in small groups to deal with immediate, pressing problems. Within a year's time the entire staff had become involved with each other and with the success of the school. Teachers enjoyed more openness and freedom with each other, with the children, and with the principal. Staff turnover, once nearly 100 per cent, was drastically reduced. At present there is a coordinating team of five teachers with special training in self-assessment, human relations, and institutional change.

In a large eastern city the same principles operate in a less formal way. One of the major sources of innovation in the school system comes from teachers who are wives of university faculty. These women are able to experiment and take risks because they have widespread, firm, and continuing support from the university community—a built-in, informal support group. As a result, one major source of stimulation in the surrounding public schools comes from these teachers.

GOALS OF THE GROUP

The basis of a small support group is simple. Six to ten teachers agree to meet on a regular basis to look more realistically and objectively at their teaching. They examine their own behavior in the light of their professional goals and direct their energies toward solving their immediate teaching problems. Eventually they begin to plan larger strategies for a more fresh, involving, and productive educational enterprise.

Groups must be designed around mutual support, not evaluation. Feedback is descriptive, and nonevaluative. Members learn how to assess *themselves*, not each other. Thus, teachers with a variety of objectives and teaching styles can feel that the group supports individual differences. Teachers of mathematics and English often think they have little in common but soon discover that they have much to share and learn from each other.

WHO SHOULD PARTICIPATE?

The composition of the first group is critical to the success of the program. Members should be open, sensitive, supportive, and professionally competent. Disgruntled, unconstructive radicals (whatever their age) tend to be unsupportive of individual differences; their criticism of the system and of individuals is rarely productive, and they often lack wisdom in their choice of battleground. Highly alienated teachers may be enthusiastic about innovation but also may be disruptive. Incompetent teachers who are struggling to survive are unprepared to deal with self-actualization needs, and they would pose especially difficult problems for a beginning group. Likewise you should probably avoid teachers who talk a game that is very different from the one they play. One example is the teacher who is rigid about his flexibility. It is almost impossible to find teachers who openly characterize themselves as narrow and rigid, but there are plenty around who say in effect, "I'm open, honest, and flexible; and God help anyone who suggests otherwise."

It would be wiser for you to hand-pick the first members rather than rely on bulletin board announcements. In this way you will minimize the initial problems in developing a climate of continuing support and efficient problem solving. On occasion you may find it helpful to invite other supportive and resourceful members of the community to attend specific meetings. Don't overlook the contributions you can get from students, administrators, board members, parents, and faculty of nearby colleges, even though they would not normally become continuing members of your group.

WHAT CAN WE TALK ABOUT?

The success of your group requires a firm agreement about objectives and procedures. If you agree to work systematically toward specific tasks, you can avoid the danger of degenerating into another series of gripe sessions or potentially destructive confrontations. I feel that amateur therapy and sensitivity training are inadequate substitutes for task-oriented problem solving.

Problem solving is the heart of the program. A problem arises when there is a discrepancy between what *is* and what *should be*, and problem solving consists in moving from where you *are* to where you *want to be*. The more specific the problem, the better; you will find it more profitable to discuss Tom's restlessness in class than to discuss how to maintain order in the classroom.

Productive problem solving discussions usually dwell on one or more of the following:

Discover your strengths and weaknesses as a professional. You can look realistically and objectively at your own performance in many ways without the aid of an observer or evaluator. Teachers most frequently use standard achievement tests, student questionnaires, videotape, and interaction analysis; Goldhammer's immensely readable *Clinical Supervision* may also be helpful. The important thing is to assess where you are as a professional and share that assessment with the group.

Clarify your professional objectives. The group is an excellent place to develop and test your image of what you would like to be. Other members can also help you describe in behavioral terms what you want for yourself, your students, and for the school system.

Identify helping and hindering forces. One of the most productive methods of planning for change is to use force-field analysis. Briefly, this means that in a stable system the forces for producing change are equally offset by forces opposed to change. It is essential to pinpoint all of the possible helping and hindering forces, so that you can take concrete steps to increase the power of the helping forces and decrease the opposition of the hindering forces. This disruption of the balance of forces results in progress toward change.

For example, the forces which might foster the development of a film program might be:

1. Your own enthusiasm.
2. Student desire for movies.
3. Available plans for beginning a film program.
4. Several receptive teachers in different disciplines.
5. Nearby schools which have used film successfully.
6. A public library willing to purchase short films.
7. Ingenuity in getting around the constraints of the system.

Forces restraining the development of a film program might be:

1. Skepticism among Old Guard teachers.
2. An overcrowded curriculum.

3. Scarcity of funds.
4. Antiquated equipment.
5. Tight schedule.
6. Worry among parents that their children won't learn any-thing.
7. The principal's belief that movies are only entertainment.

There are many ways to proceed in such a situation, the most readily apparent being to design proposals for developing a film program by drawing upon available literature and the existing program in the neighboring school, and to present it to various departments, the principal, and the curriculum committee. A po-tentially effective complementary approach, however, might be to involve the skeptics, the principal, and influential parents in some informal film classes, examine the results with them, plan next steps, and begin a small support group among film study enthu-siasts. Another strategy might be to initiate a re-examination of the schedule, involving all gatekeepers, and thereby begin a parallel effort for change.

It is true that if you consider film important enough, you can find ways to use it, but you are not likely to produce significant change by ingenuity alone. By working toward widespread but specific change, such as development of alternative scheduling patterns, you can address school-wide concerns while promoting your own program.

Select relevant resources. In order to accomplish your pur-poses more effectively you may need to draw upon the resources of others. There is no value in change for the sake of change. Change is productive when it is relevant to your own needs and goals. The group can share the expertise of all its members and can gain access to additional material and human resources. Experiment with new behavior and report your results to the group.

Explore concepts and philosophy of education. There is now an extensive literature which deals with innovation and education-al change (see Appendix II). Your efforts will be more rewarding if they develop within sound conceptual guidelines.

At the same time, it is important that you design ways to practice what you preach. It is difficult to find a school, depart-mental curriculum, or group of teachers without a philosophy most educators would generally endorse. However, what teachers do and use in the classroom often contradict that philosophy. One of the most useful tasks a group can help you perform is to design ways to carry out your educational convictions. Behavioral objec-tives can be helpful up to a point, but applying value clarification procedures to your own teaching and personal behavior in a supportive climate and solving problems is even more pertinent.[1]

Critique the function of your support group. Some time may be profitably spent in looking at how your group is working together. You can apply force-field analysis to your group meetings and devise ways of maximizing what is helpful and eliminating what is unsupportive or irrelevant.

WHERE CAN WE GO FOR HELP?

In addition to calling on outside resources in the community, perhaps in a nearby college, and studying the literature on change, you can also reinforce the group by affiliating in some way with individuals and groups across the country. In Chicago, for instance, film teachers have banded together throughout the metropolitan area in the Screen Educators Society, whose magazine, *See*, is one of the best recent resources for film teachers. New York City has a similar group called MAFIA (Metropolitan Area Film Instructors Association). The support group need not confine its attention to film, of course, for there are many paths to creating a climate of freedom in schools. The key is to identify and communicate regularly with supportive individuals and groups in your own informal network.

The group can also enlist the support of students, who can become important allies for promoting planned change. Using your support group as a model, students can form their own small groups, perhaps inviting an adult to facilitate, in order to plan their own methods of behaving more effectively in school to create the kind of climate and programs they would like to have.

Since I have said a great deal about taking direct action, I will now provide a concrete chance to take one. The last page of this book is a form for you to fill out if you wish. It is a checklist that asks a few direct, simple questions about what actions you have taken, not what actions you intend to take. Look it over as a set of guidelines for getting started, and when you have started to move, fill it out and send it to me, in care of the publisher, and we can begin our own network.

This device will help me, too, for I have discovered that everything exciting that has happened to me has come as a result

---

[1]See Raths, Louis, Merrill Harmin, and Sidney Simon: *Values and Teaching.* Columbus, Ohio: Charles E. Merrill Co. Publishers, 1966.

of building on relationships with people I have met by chance. For that reason I go out of my way to attend meetings, conventions, and schools where I am likely to run into interesting people. I believe that I can gain a great deal of support and stimulation from my own far-flung network of good people. I would like to extend it here and now, and I hereby offer to join yours.

I hope this book has given you some good ideas you will want to build upon, but I also hope this book helps me find you. Carl Rogers has written that one of the most satisfying experiences for him is to really *hear* someone, and to feel that he has been heard. As an author, I too would like to feel heard. If you respond, you can be sure I'll listen.

APPENDIX I

Books on Film, Film Study, and Closely Related Topics

Agee, James: *Agee on Film: Reviews and Comments.* Boston: Beacon Press, 1964 (paper).

Arlen, Michael J.: *Living Room War.* New York: The Viking Press, Inc., 1969.

Arnheim, Rudolf: *Film As Art.* Berkeley: University of California Press, 1967.

Bluestone, George: *Novels Into Film.* Berkeley: University of California Press, 1961 (paper).

Bobker, Lee R.: *Elements of Film.* New York: Harcourt Brace Jovanovich, Inc., 1969 (paper).

Brodbeck, Emil E.: *Handbook of Basic Motion Picture Techniques.* New York: American Photographic Book Publishing Co., Inc., 1969.

Crowther, Bosley: *The Great Films.* New York: G. P. Putnam's Sons, 1967.

Durgnat, Raymond: *Films and Feelings.* Cambridge: The M.I.T. Press, 1967.

Eisenstein, Sergei: *Film Form and the Film Sense.* Cleveland: Meridan Books, 1957 (paper).

Fulton, Albert R.: *Motion Pictures: The Development of an Art From the Silent Films to the Age of Television.* Norman: University of Oklahoma Press, 1960.

Hodgkinson, Anthony: *Screen Education.* New York: UNESCO Publication Center, 1963.

Huss, Roy, and N. Silverstein: *The Film Experience: Elements of Motion Picture Art.* New York: Harper & Row, Publishers, 1966.

Jacobs, Lewis: *The Rise of the American Film,* 3rd ed. New York: Teachers College Press, 1968.

Kael, Pauline: *I Lost It At The Movies.* New York: Bantam Books, 1965 (paper).

Kael, Pauline: *Kiss Kiss, Bang Bang.* New York: Bantam Books, 1969 (paper).

Knight, Arthur: *The Liveliest Art.* New York: The New American Library, Inc., 1957 (paper).

Kuhns, William, and R. Stanley: *Exploring the Film.* Dayton: George A. Pflaum, Publisher, 1968.

Lindgren, Ernest: *The Art of the Film.* New York: The Macmillan Company, 1962.

Lowndes, Douglas: *Film Making In Schools.* New York: Watson-Guptill Publications, 1968.

MacCann, Richard Dyer: *A Montage of Theories.* New York: E. P. Dutton & Co., Inc., 1966.

Mallery, David: *The School and the Art of Motion Pictures.* Revised ed. Boston: National Association of Independent Schools, 1965 (paper).

Mallery, David: *Film in the Life of the School.* Boston: National Association of Independent Schools, 1968 (paper).

Sarris, Andrew: *The American Cinema: Directors and Directions: 1929-1968.* New York: E. P. Dutton & Co., Inc., 1968 (paper).

Sohn, David: *Film Study and the English Teacher.* Bloomington: Field Services, Indiana University Audio-Visual Center, 1968 (paper).

Stephenson, Ralph, and J. R. Debrix: *The Cinema as Art.* Baltimore: Penguin Books, Inc., 1965 (paper).

Sullivan, Sister Bede: *Movies, The Universal Language.* South Bend: Fides Publishers, Inc., 1967 (paper).

APPENDIX II

The Literature on Change, and References for Support Groups

Amidon, E. J., and N. A. Flanders: *The Role of the Teacher in the Classroom.* Minneapolis: Association for Productive Teaching, Inc., 1967.

Benne, K. D., and Bozidar Muntyan (Eds.): *Human Relations in Curriculum Change.* New York: The Dryden Press, 1951.

Culbertson, Jack (Ed.): Changing the schools. *Theory Into Practice,* Vol. 11, No. 5, December, 1963.

Eisner, Elliott W.: Educational objectives: Help or hindrance? *School Review,* 75:250-282, 1967.

Eisner, Elliott W.: The new rationality in art education. Speech given at the AERA conference, New York City, February, 1969.

Furbay, Albert: Material available in mimeograph from author. Furbay is Associate Professor of Speech and Communications, Western Michigan University, Kalamazoo, Michigan, 49001.

Goldhammer, Robert: *Clinical Supervision.* New York: Holt, Rinehart & Winston, Inc., 1969.

Havelock, Ronald G.: *A Guide to Innovation in Education.* Ann Arbor: Institute for Social Research, The University of Michigan, 1970.

Leonard, George: *Education and Ecstasy.* New York: Dell Publishing Company, Inc., 1969.

Lippitt, Ronald, Jeanne Watson, and Bruce Westley: *The Dynamics of Planned Change.* New York: Harcourt Brace Jovanovich, Inc., 1958.

Mager, Robert F.: *Preparing Instructional Objectives.* Palo Alto: Fearon Publishers, 1962.

Miles, Matthew (Ed): *Innovation in Education.* New York: Teachers College Press, 1964.

National Association of Secondary School Principals: Changing secondary schools. *The Bulletin,* Vol. 47, No. 283, May, 1963.

Phillips, Mark: Teaching American history with the 3 Little Pigs. *Media and Methods,* December, 1969, pp. 65-86.

Polanyi, Michael: *Personal Knowledge.* New York: Harper and Row, Publishers, 1964.

Postman, Neil, and Charles Weingartner: *Teaching as a Subversive Activity.* New York: Dell Publishing Co., Inc., 1969.

Raths, Louis, Merrill Harmin, and Sidney Simon: *Values and Teaching.* Columbus, Ohio: Charles E. Merrill Publishers, 1966.

Rogers, Carl: *Freedom To Learn.* Columbus, Ohio: Charles E. Merrill Publishers, 1969.

Schein, E. H., and W. G. Bennis: *Personal and Organizational Change Through Group Methods.* New York: John Wiley & Sons, Inc., 1967.

Schmuck, Richard, and Ronald Lippitt: *Problem Solving To Improve Classroom Learning.* Chicago: Science Research Associates, 1967.

Snyder, Ben: Upward-Bound and A-Better Chance Programs at the movies. The Independent School Bulletin, Vol. 27, No. 3, February, 1968, p. 74.

Taylor, Harold: *Art and the Intellect.* New York: Doubleday & Company, Inc., 1968.

Watson, Goodwin (Ed.): *Concepts for Social Change.* Cooperative Project for Educational Development by the National Training Laboratories, National Education Association, Washington, D.C., 1967 (Order from NTL, NEA, 1201 16th St., N.W., Washington, D.C., $2.50).

APPENDIX III

PERIODICALS ON FILM AND FILM STUDY

Catholic Film Newsletter
635 Madison Avenue
New York, New York
10022

Cinema
9641 Santa Monica Boulevard
Beverly Hills, California
90210

Film Comment
11 St. Luke's Place
New York, New York
10014

Film News
250 W. 57th St.
New York, New York
10019

Film Quarterly
University of California Press
Berkeley, California
94704

Media and Methods
134 N. 13th St.
Philadelphia, Pennsylvania
19107

Screen Education
c/o School of Public
    Communications
Boston University
Boston, Massachusetts
02115

See
George Pflaum Publishing Co.,
    Inc., and Screen Educators
    Society
38 W. Fifth St.
Dayton, Ohio
45402

Sight and Sound
255 Seventh Avenue
New York, New York
10001

Take One
Unicorn Publishing Corp.
P.O. Box 1778
Station B
Montreal, 10, Canada

APPENDIX IV

DISTRIBUTORS OF FILMS MENTIONED IN TEXT

FILM	DISTRIBUTOR
Allures	Janus Films
An American Time Capsule	Pathe-Contemporary Films, Inc. (c/o McGraw-Hill)
An Occurrence at Owl Creek Bridge	Pathe-Contemporary Films, Inc. (c/o McGraw-Hill)
Boundary Lines	Pathe-Contemporary Films, Inc. (c/o McGraw-Hill)
Castro Street	Filmmakers Cooperative
Cattle Ranch	Pathe-Contemporary Films, Inc. (c/o McGraw-Hill)
Children Adrift	Stuart Reynolds Productions
Clay	Pathe-Contemporary Films, Inc. (c/o McGraw-Hill)
Corral	Pathe-Contemporary Films, Inc. (c/o McGraw-Hill)
David and Lisa	Walter Reade 16
Dream of the Wild Horses	Pathe-Contemporary Films, Inc. (c/o McGraw-Hill)
Eye of the Beholder	Stuart Reynolds Productions
Fail Safe	Brandon Films, Inc.
Glass	Pathe-Contemporary Films, Inc. (c/o McGraw-Hill)
Harvest of Shame	Pathe-Contemporary Films, Inc. (c/o McGraw-Hill)
Help! My Snowman's Burning	Pathe-Contemporary Films, Inc. (c/o McGraw-Hill)
High School	OSTI

FILM	DISTRIBUTOR
Hunger in America	Carousel Films, Inc.
Judoka	Pathe-Contemporary Films, Inc. (c/o McGraw-Hill)
King Kong	Brandon Films, Inc.
Leaf	Pyramid Films
Man of Aran	Pathe-Contemporary Films, Inc. (c/o McGraw-Hill)
Nanook of the North	Pathe-Contemporary Films, Inc. (c/o McGraw-Hill)
Neighbors	Pathe-Contemporary Films, Inc. (c/o McGraw-Hill)
No Reason To Stay	Pathe-Contemporary Films, Inc. (c/o McGraw-Hill) and Films, Inc.
N.Y., N.Y.	Francis Thompson, Inc.
On the Waterfront	Brandon Films, Inc., Pathe-Contemporary Films, Inc., (c/o McGraw-Hill) *and* Twyman Films, Inc.
Orange	Filmmakers Cooperative
Pacific 231	Pathe-Contemporary Films, Inc. (c/o McGraw-Hill)
Pigs!	Churchill Films
Point of Order!	Walter Reade 16
Rhinoceros	Pathe-Contemporary Films, Inc. (c/o McGraw-Hill)
Run!	Brandon Films, Inc.
Sky	Pathe-Contemporary Films, Inc. (c/o McGraw-Hill)
Tamer of Wild Horses	Pathe-Contemporary Films, Inc. (c/o McGraw-Hill)
The Anderson Platoon	Pathe-Contemporary Films, Inc. (c/o McGraw-Hill)

FILM	DISTRIBUTOR
The Battle of Culloden	Time-Life Films
The Critic	Pathe-Contemporary Films, Inc. (c/o McGraw-Hill)
The Exiles	Pathe-Contemporary Films, Inc. (c/o McGraw-Hill)
The Hand	Pathe-Contemporary Films, Inc. (c/o McGraw-Hill)
The Heart Is a Lonely Hunter	Warner Brothers
The Loneliness of the Long Distance Runner	Walter Reade 16
The Responsive Eye	Pathe-Contemporary Films, Inc. (c/o McGraw-Hill)
The Student	Pathe-Contemporary Films, Inc. (c/o McGraw-Hill)
The Three Little Pigs	Audio Film Center (Cartoon Parade #8)
The Wild One	Trans-World Films, Inc., *and* Twyman Films, Inc.
3:10 to Yuma	Pathe-Contemporary Films, Inc. (c/o McGraw-Hill)
Time Piece	Pathe-Contemporary Films, Inc. (c/o McGraw-Hill)
Toys	Pathe-Contemporary Films, Inc. (c/o McGraw-Hill)
Triumph of the Will	Museum of Modern Art
Very Nice, Very Nice	Pathe-Contemporary Films, Inc. (c/o McGraw-Hill)

APPENDIX V

Films often change hands or can be found at more than one distributor. Also, libraries usually have a good stock of short films.

Aci Films, Inc.
16 W. 46th St.
New York, New York
10036

Alden Films
5113 16th Avenue
Brooklyn, New York
11204

American Film Registry
831 S. Wabash Avenue
Chicago, Illinois
60605

*American Television
Commercials Festival*
6 W. 57th St.
New York, New York
10019

Association Films
600 Madison Avenue
New York, New York
10022

Audio Film Center
10 Fiske Place
Mount Vernon, New York
10550
  Midwest office:
    2138 E. 75th St.
    Chicago, Illinois
    60649

West Coast office:
  406 Clement Street
  San Francisco, California
  94118

Brandon Films, Inc.
221 W. 57th St.
New York, New York
10019
  Film Center, Inc.
  20 E. Huron St.
  Chicago, Illinois
  60611
  Western Cinema Guild, Inc.
  244 Kearny St.
  San Francisco, California
  94108

Capitol Films
309 N. Thirteenth St.
Philadelphia, Pennsylvania
19107

Carousel Films, Inc.
1501 Broadway
New York, New York
10036

Churchill Films
662 N. Robertson Boulevard
Los Angeles, California
90069

Cinema Guild
10 Fiske Place
Mount Vernon, New York
10050

Cinema 16
234 Lexington Avenue
New York, New York
10016

College Film Center
See Trans-World Films, Inc.

Columbia Cinemateque
111 Fifth Avenue
New York, New York
10022

Consort-Orion Films
116 E. 60th St.
New York, New York
10022

Contemporary Films
330 W. 42nd St.
New York, New York
10036
  Midwest office:
    828 Custer Avenue
    Evanston, Illinois
    60202
  West Coast office:
    1211 Polk St.
    San Francisco, California
    94109

Economy Film Library
4336 Sunset Boulevard
Los Angeles, California
90028

Embassy Pictures Corp.
1301 Avenue of the Americas
New York, New York
10019

Fiesta Films, Inc.
7303 W. 55th Pl.
Summit, Illinois
60501

Filmmakers Cooperative
414 Park Avenue South
New York, New York
10016

Films, Inc.
  Home office:
    425 N. Michigan Avenue
    Chicago, Illinois
    60611

  Branch offices:
    5625 Hollywood
      Boulevard
    Hollywood, California
    90028
    Serving Arizona,
      California, Colorado, Hawaii,
      Nevada, and Wyoming

  277 Pharr Road N.E.
  Atlanta, Georgia
  30305

  161 Massachusetts Avenue
  Boston, Massachusetts
  02115

  2639 Grand River
  Detroit, Michigan
  48240

38 W. 32nd St.
New York, New York
10001

2129 N.E. Broadway
Portland, Oregon
97212
Also serving Alaska

1414 Dragon Street
Dallas, Texas
75207

Desert Book Co.
44 East South Temple
Salt Lake City, Utah
84111

Francis Thompson, Inc.
231 E. 51st St.
New York, New York
10022

Harrison Pictures
1501 Broadway
New York, New York
10036

Ideal Pictures
1010 Church St.
Evanston, Illinois
60201

*Institutional Cinema Service,
Inc.*
29 E. 10th St.
New York, New York
10003

International Film Bureau
332 S. Michigan Avenue
Chicago, Illinois
60604

Irving Lesser Enterprises
527 Madison Avenue
New York, New York
10022

I. Q. Films
Robert Saudek Associates
689 Fifth Avenue
New York, New York
10022

Jan-Or Pictures, Inc.
890 Napoli Drive
Pacific Palisades, California
90272

Janus Films
24 W. 58th St.
New York, New York
10019

Mass Media Ministries
2116 N. Charles St.
Baltimore, Maryland
21218

Modern Sound Pictures
1410 Howard Street
Omaha, Nebraska
68102

Museum of Modern Art
11 W. 53rd St.
New York, New York
10019

National Film Board of
Canada
680 Fifth Avenue
New York, New York
10019

OSTI
(Headed by Frederick
Wiseman)
Cambridge, Massachusetts

Pathe-Contemporary Films,
Inc.
c/o McGraw-Hill Book
Company
330 W. 42nd St.
New York, New York
10036

Pictura Films
41 Union Square, West
New York, New York
10003

Pyramid Films
Box 1048
Santa Monica, California
90406

Radim Films
220 W. 42nd St.
New York, New York
10036

Stuart Reynolds Productions
9465 Wilshire Boulevard
Beverly Hills, California
90212

Swank Motion Pictures, Inc.
201 S. Jefferson St.
St. Louis, Missouri
63103

Teaching Film Custodians,
Inc.
25 W. 43rd St.
New York, New York
10036

"The" Film Center
915 Twelfth St., N.W.
Washington, D.C.
20005

Time-Life Films
43 W. 16th St.
New York, New York
10011

Trans-World Films, Inc.
McCormick Building,
Room 528
332 S. Michigan Ave.
Chicago, Illinois
60604
Also: College Film Center,
same address.

Twyman Films, Inc.
329 Salem Avenue
Dayton, Ohio
45401

United Artists 16
729 Seventh Avenue
New York, New York
10019

United World Films
Branch offices:
1025 N. Highland Avenue
Los Angles, California
90038

287 Techwood Drive, N.W.
Atlanta, Georgia
30313

425 N. Michigan Avenue
Chicago, Illinois
60611

221 Park Avenue S.
New York, New York
10003

5023 N.E. Sandy
   Boulevard
Portland, Oregon
97213

6434 Maple Avenue
Dallas, Texas
75235

Walter Reade 16
241 E. 34th St.
New York, New York
10016

Warner Brothers
4000 Warner Boulevard
Burbank, California
91503

APPENDIX VI

Mail to:
Richard Lacey   Date _____
c/o Education Editor
W. B. Saunders Company
West Washington Square
Philadelphia, Pennsylvania
19105

Name:

Address:

School:

I am a _____.

_____ I'm in a support group.

_____ I'm into the reading.

This is what I want to say to you: